fragile

fragile

NIKI SHISLER

EBURY
PRESS

3 5 7 9 10 8 6 4 2

This edition published in 2007

First published in 2006 by Ebury Press, an imprint of Ebury Publishing

Ebury Publishing is a division of the Random House Group

The Random House Group Limited Reg. No. 954009

Addresses for companies within the Random House Group
can be found at www.randomhouse.co.uk

A CIP catalogue record for this book is available from the British Library

The Random House Group Limited makes every effort to ensure that
the papers used in our books are made from trees that have been legally
sourced from well-managed and credibly certified forests. Our paper
procurement policy can be found on www.randomhouse.co.uk

Printed and bound in Great Britain by
Cox & Wyman Ltd, Reading, Berkshire

ISBN: 9780091910006

For my incredible husband Danny,
who took every step of this journey with me.

acknowledgements

This was always going to be a long list; a life like mine doesn't happen without copious amounts of help. Inevitably, there will be names missed out; restrictions of space make it impossible for me to individually mention all the people who have supported me and my family through the writing of this book.

First thanks go to Doug Young, the person who nudged me into actually taking myself and my story seriously. Doug also pointed me at my wonderful agent, Clare Alexander at Gillon Aitken, who provided support and encouragement in my flustered and nervy early days. Fiona MacIntyre at Ebury Press has been my editor and so much more; providing a calm and guiding hand for this somewhat high-maintenance writer, invaluable advice and a working relationship that has been warm, easy and productive. The more I learn about the publishing business, the more I realise how lucky I've been to have Clare and Fiona on my team; it really has been a privilege and a pleasure to learn from two women who I respect so much. Nikki Bailey read the manuscript, made constructive criticisms and gave great advice; and Barbara Boosfeld checked the entire book for medical accuracy: the end product is much better for both their input. Thanks also to everyone at Century for looking after me so beautifully while I wrote, especially the staff of the 1st floor bar, who must have thought I'd taken root at the corner table.

Eamonn Forde and Beverley Marsland both read, chapter-by-chapter, as I was writing it. They kept me connected to an audience as well as regular coffee and lunch dates. Without their ability to stick with me, I would probably have finished this project entirely friendless. Linda Levy has supported me as a writer and a friend for many years now, and is one of the few people outside my family, who has borne close witness to this story from its earliest days. Alev Adil, my oldest friend and an incredible writer herself, gave me advice and confidence in my own ability as, indeed, she has done since our schooldays together.

Through my internet connection, I have 'met' countless other parents and my online relationships have been a key part of this journey, and this book. To the families of the Twins List who carried me through my darkest days: my debt to you is immeasurable. You were there, you know what it meant; consider this book my tribute to the love I was shown. I could not possibly mention everyone but I need to single out Tracey Scow who, literally, crossed oceans to hold my hand during the worst times. David McDougal and The Nemaline Myopathy group have been a source of support, advice, information and friendship. You guys are like family to me; the group is incredibly special and I'm really proud to be a part of it. My final 'group hug' goes out to Randy

Ryan and the families of Our-Kids, who have provided me with information, entertainment and a space to let off steam: thank you all for keeping me sane.

My home life has continued to tick over, despite me being preoccupied with this project for the best part of a year, because of the incredible support I get at home. Camden Primary Care Trust have been fantastic; their Paediatric Community Nursing Team in particular is a great example of what the NHS, at its best, can achieve. Again, there are far too many names for me to list them all, but Lynda Horsman stands out as someone who has gone above and beyond the call of duty many times. Medical matters aside, my domestic life would crumble without my amazing childminder/au-pair/friend Draga, who 'mothers' us all and stops us from dissolving into chaos.

My family. To the whole Shisler/Shaw family but especially Pauline, Anne and Geoffrey, and Abi and Ben Warren, thank you for your generosity in allowing me to share what is your story as well as mine; I know it has not always been easy for you. I hope that you feel this book justifies your trust; please know it is written with the utmost love and respect for you all. To the Condou family – Mama, Pierre, Charlie: I love you all more than I can say, thank you for being there always. This has been *our* journey and we have come through it, as we always do, together. Thank you, thank you, thank you.

And finally, my children. Joey, Evie and Felix: the purest happiness I have ever known has come from you. I am so proud of you all and your astonishing spirits; you are my strength and my inspiration. I love you.

~ 1 ~

What's the worst that could happen? Seriously. Where does your darkest fear lie? The one that knots your gut, that you push from your mind with a silent prayer and a shudder. Probably your loved ones feature: your partner, friends, parents. Or, more likely, your children.

Bad things happen to good people just as often as good things happen to bad people and, more to the point, incredible things happen to average people. All my life I felt I was 'different'; it took being catapulted, without warning, into an extraordinary life, to show me how fundamentally normal I was. I don't have all the answers. I am, like most people, only doing the best I can; putting one foot in front of the other and trying to look like I know where I'm going. An ordinary woman, trying to make sense of a life that often seems senseless; some days are better than others. I used to think that adulthood would bring a sense of certainty to life; two solid feet planted firmly on stable ground. But I have found that the earth never stops shifting and moving beneath us, we just acquire the skill to keep from stumbling at every tremor. Life is *so* precarious; I'm not talking about the actual breath of life although, God knows, that's fragile enough too. No, I mean the living of life; the daily tightrope-walk where anything is possible and we are never more than a heartbeat away from elation or despair.

I have asked the big questions of my life. Who am I? What am I? Why? As chaos has trundled noisily across my world I have grabbed at straws of meaning, looking for patterns, for something to guide me. I have found no shortage of answers, both physical and spiritual; there are a thousand ways to tell the story of the journey from cradle to grave. For me though, the arc of my life is best described through the points where it touches others. This is where I exist; where I become real. Alone, I am wraith-like, insubstantial and impotent, weaving a traceless route through the days.

But, of course, I am not alone. There are so many other lives intertwined with mine, and each one sends a ripple through the universe, criss-crossing with all the other ripples from a million other touches. I need touch and I need intimacy, despite my frequent difficulty with social interaction; so I have learned to reach out and to make connections with people in different ways. It seems that, even in the most trying times, we will always find ways to touch each other, to share our stories and our souls because, when all is said and done, what else is there? What else really counts in life? We need to belong to each other, to anchor ourselves in the web of relationships; so we build our networks, our families, and we risk our hearts because that is what makes a life.

Happiness is an art; a skill to master like any other. It has taken me more than forty years to learn this; wisdom better late than never.

* * *

It's a typical term-time morning in my house. Chaos. There are, on average, eight people milling around in various states of coherence, from super-zingy awakeness to near-coma. Introductions: let's start with Danny. My husband/friend/soulmate/lover, my co-traveller and also the Voice of Reason. Danny is probably the sanest person I know: balanced, kind, tolerant, loving and rational. How he ended up here with me I will never know, but there is not a day that goes by without me marvelling at my luck and sending grateful thoughts out into the universe. We are a good team; we seem to suit each other. Danny and I never argue, a fact that many people find deeply suspicious and which, even I admit, is unusual to the point of being bizarre. However, as will become abundantly clear, I am no Stepford spouse and Danny is far from being a doormat; we just don't fight. I love Danny with everything I am, every cell in my body is plumply satisfied by my love for my husband and, even after almost ten years, I am hard pushed to find fault in him. Sickening, isn't it? And yet once you have read our story, seen the mountains we have had to climb, I think you won't begrudge us this one area of smugness.

Mornings do not find Danny at his most efficient. In life I am mostly chaos, with occasional bursts of Nazi-like organisational fervour, but Danny bumbles through the first hour of the day before mutating into a bright and personable human being. So, for the purposes of this introduction, we meet him absent-mindedly pushing a small foot into a smaller sock or vaguely searching for a hairbrush and trying to at least *look* useful.

Did you see that? Perhaps, just out of the corner of your eye, you noticed something that looked a little like an overloaded coat rack scurry across the hall and out of the door. That will have been Joey; my firstborn child. Only eighteen years old and yet he's already seen more life action than your average pensioner. He, rather wisely, makes great efforts to avoid any contact with the rest of us until post meridian. He is a heroic big brother to his siblings; an endless source of entertainment, education and adventure. Joey was never very good at being a child; he deeply resented the powerlessness and was kicking against being patronised from around the age of two. Fortunately he has grown into himself beautifully and continually astounds me with his general 'great kid-ness'. He's funny, smart, talented and kind, everything that a mother could wish for; and, I'm sure I need hardly tell you, I say all this without the slightest hint of bias or partiality.

The star of our family show is, undoubtedly, Evie. Seven going on seventeen (Joey wanted a teenage sibling, and now he has created one), she, in complete contrast to her older brother, has settled into childhood like a pro. Pretty, popular, super-girly and entirely in tune with the playground zeitgeist; mornings find her well-rested and raring to go. It's a busy time of day for her; she has to find a way to squeeze eating breakfast and arguing about her outfit into an already packed schedule which includes dancing like a pop star, practising juggling, downloading screensavers from Barbie.com, writing letters, answering emails, fighting with her siblings over the Playstation, watching TV and asking questions like 'what *is* philosophy?' All accompanied by a stream-of-consciousness running commentary aimed at nobody and everybody. Evie is a gorgeous kid with a heart of gold and a mind like a razor; she is also exhausting, her skinny little body containing more energy than the rest of the family combined, and it is a rare morning that doesn't involve someone yelling at her (in a loving way, naturally).

If we are moving chronologically, we should meet Theo next, but Theo is no longer here, at least not in any physical sense. Certainly his influence remains, the fact of his having once lived shapes our family as much as any of his still-breathing siblings; and, though he is still sorely missed, only the preternaturally observant would notice the little Theo-shaped hole in our life.

Just two minutes younger than Theo is the baby of the family, six-year-old Felix. Fee's got more baggage than an airport carousel, both literally and metaphorically, and, on first meeting, is an arresting sight. It's difficult to know where to start when describing him; it's not easy for me to see him anew, through your eyes. Felix is physically disabled. He has a condition called Nemaline Myopathy, a muscle disorder that makes him profoundly weak. All those bodily functions that most of us take for granted are much more difficult for him. Felix needs help to breathe, to swallow, to do countless things that should be reflexive. His body piercings are rather more radical than those of even the wildest Hell's Angel: a tracheostomy studs his neck and another tube (his gastrostomy) decorates his tummy and enables him to be fed. He receives all his meals this way, bypassing his mouth entirely. From his trach, there snakes a long tube which connects him permanently and continuously to a ventilator; the air around him hums slightly with the gentle buzzing of the machinery and the *swoosh* of the air with each breath. By now you're probably imagining my boy as frail and sickly; perhaps even envisaging a mini intensive-care unit in my home, with people speaking in hushed tones and a medical chart hooked to the end of the bed. If you are, then you are certainly in good company. I am used to these assumptions having heard them not just from lay people, who can hardly be expected to know any differently, but also from countless doctors, who remain astonishingly ignorant of what can be achieved outside a hospital setting.

In fact Felix is bright-eyed, full of life, spirit and knock-out charm. My only fair child, his dirty-blond hair stands to attention in clusters of unruly tufts. He drives a power-wheelchair with his portable ventilator and battery bolted to its back. He can drive with extraordinary skill that is, unfortunately, unmatched by any sense of caution or concern for life, limb or property. Despite the ability to perform the world's tightest three-point turn and to negotiate a complex path backwards and at speed, he has still managed to take one door off its hinges, and leave a footplate-height scuff-mark running the full length of every single wall in the house.

Felix can't talk, or rather he can't talk in a way that many people can understand. His muscle weakness means that even though he can make sounds, he cannot articulate them clearly into words. Physically, he can't actually close his mouth, so this alone rules out a large chunk of the alphabet. He signs a bit and has a good shot at talking but we know that eventually a Stephen Hawking-style artificial voice is likely to be his best option.

Felix's condition also accounts for several more of the people that can be found depleting oxygen levels in my home. Being on a ventilator full-time (or 'technology dependent', to use the modern parlance) entitles Felix to round-the-clock nursing support. The day and night shifts change over at eight o'clock and, when you include the inevitable student or trainee, this adds another three bodies, on average, to the mix.

And what about me? Well, I'm a writer. Perhaps it seems superfluous to tell you that: you are, after all, holding a book with my name on the front. But in this age of me-me-me celebrity, where everyone seems to have a story to share and the world is full of victims, it's probably worth pointing out that this is not a ghost-written 'My True Story'; it is what I do. I write. I have always written and, until blindness or dementia claim me, I presume I always will. The story you are going to read, that I am going to tell, is as much about the fact that I am a writer as it is about the dramatic chain of events that unfolded. I am not particularly good with people; small talk is an alien concept to me and I often feel awkward and tongue-tied in company. Unfortunately, this innate difficulty with social niceties is not matched by a commensurate desire to be silent. No, quite the reverse. You want an opinion? No problem! No subject is too large or too small; I can deliver you an ill-thought-out analysis, with passion and conviction, virtually on-demand. So, naturally, I became a writer.

I have a history, and it's not particularly pretty. I have been in recovery from alcoholism for ten years now and my journey to the rooms of AA was as sordid and uncomfortable as you might imagine. I have, as they say, been around the block a few times. Why am

I telling you this? Because I want you to know that I am not any kind of saint. I am just a regular flawed person who has, over the years, demonstrated both an uncanny ability to make stupid decisions and an impressive resistance to growing up. The thing is, before the twins, I would have told you that I was not the type to do the whole special-needs thing. I saw disability as something that was reserved for the lives of wannabe martyrs; those worthy do-gooders who made cakes for the church fête, and wore unfashionable shoes. In the unlikely event of me giving any thought to such matters, I would probably have assumed that I wasn't nice enough, good enough or, quite frankly, dull enough to live with disability.

While I am, like most people, a seething mass of grisly shortcomings, there are two flaws that, I believe, stand out from the others and are prominent enough to be recognisably My Biggest Faults. Firstly, there is my inability to do anything in moderation. I'm an all-or-nothing girl even though I have learned, and usually the hard way, that moderation is an infinitely more successful life strategy. Unfortunately, knowing this is one thing; the truth is I still don't really *understand* moderation. If you're going to do a thing, why would you not want to put your heart and soul into it? And if something makes me feel good then my instinct tells me that more equals better. Despite the traumatic life lessons that have knocked me senseless too many times to recount, and despite the incontrovertible evidence of chaos and misery littering my past, like some pathetic dog that drags its mangy frame back to an abusive master *every single time* he abandons it on the motorway, I continue to sniff around excess on the off-chance that this time it won't kick me in the teeth. These days though, I'm sensible enough to limit my addictive tendencies to those mind-numbing pastimes that won't kill me: previously these have included embroidery and painting. My current obsessions are computer card games and cryptic crosswords, which I do at speeds and in numbers that awe my husband, clearly an added bonus.

My second major fault is a complete inability to multi-task; I absolutely cannot focus on more than one thing at a time. Now I expect that you can already see how this, combined with flaw number one, is going to be something of a stumbling block on the path to a productive life. Astoundingly, I have only just started to realise it (which makes my ability to do cryptic crosswords at speed look a lot less impressive). Anyway, knowledge is power supposedly and self-knowledge is the first step on the road to peace of mind or enlightenment or something.

By now, with me self-outed as anti-social, opinionated and hopelessly flaky, you are probably starting to wonder how I ever managed to get my inefficient little hooks into the saintly and God-like Danny. As I said earlier, I do marvel at my own sheer good luck most days; but obviously I cannot be entirely devoid of good points either. To counter all those ghastly shortcomings, I have one real skill. I know how to love and I do it well. I love my family beyond measure, my husband and my children, I give my heart to them completely and I try to have that love sit lightly on their shoulders, so they are not burdened by it. Love is the golden thread that runs through it all, that draws us out of the dark days and into the fluttering light. My beautiful family; unconventional, idiosyncratic, full of contradictions, fragile and strong. Bound together by love and by me, the beating heart at its centre.

~ 2 ~

The thing about hitting rock bottom is that there's really only one way to go from there. By the time I crawled into recovery, a few days after my thirty-third birthday, I was a comprehensively broken woman. As the alcoholic fog lifted, giving me my first clear-eyed view of the world for many years, it became horribly and abundantly obvious that no part of my life was undamaged. The combination of drink and despair had laid waste to my whole world and I surveyed the resultant mess with horror and shame. I'll spare you the full details of my downward spiral: the story is neither glamorous nor unusual, just another pathetically ordinary tale of alcoholic misery, tragically mundane. It could so easily have ended there, in the gutter, as it does for so many alcoholics; and I would be a fool to believe that I was somehow different from any other drunk, or immune from the darker consequences of the disease.

My eventual release came more by luck than by design. The

right word at the right time managed to find a chink in my armour of denial and hit home. With no ceremony or forethought I found myself in a taxi going to my first AA meeting, still drunk from the leftover wine I had consumed for breakfast, and clutching my mother's hand like a talisman.

The early months of recovery are bizarrely surreal and bewildering. When everything you touch and everything you do has been filtered through the anaesthetic veil of alcohol for almost twenty years, sobriety will feel nerve-janglingly harsh. Suddenly I found that I was not only having to face the grim reality of a supremely fucked-up life, but I was having to do it naked, skinned even; every tender nerve was raw and bleeding, and I lacked even the smallest sliver of cushioning or protection. I cried a lot. I wept for myself, for my son, for my family. I cried for every hurt that had been buried at the bottom of a glass, every fear, every shame; on and on, endless tears of sorrow, anger, disappointment, pain. I sobbed my way through confessional meetings and private prayers until, eventually, I'd cried enough to wash the worst of the alcoholic grime from my heart and could stand, with freshly scrubbed and scoured soul, before the mirror and not be too horrified with what I saw.

I stepped out into this brave new sober life kitten-weak, wide-eyed and bewildered, and yet filled with incredible joy. It was as though I had been blind and then, having learned to cope with my disability, to read Braille and to feel my way gingerly through life; I had discovered that *Hallelujah*! It turns out that I had simply neglected to turn on the light. It was so simple; so stupidly, comically, beautifully simple: how could I not have known?

This rebirth, this fresh-sheet, clean-slate, start-again dawn is perhaps the closest I have ever come to actual light-heartedness. Optimism bubbled through me and made me tingle and, after decades of searching for the perfect drug kick, I discovered that no narcotic on earth even came close to the feeling of being high on hope. Most importantly, having snatched sweet, liberating victory from the snapping jaws of defeat, I was seized with the joyful real-isation that anything was possible and everything was repairable. I was getting another chance and, after years of ever-decreasing choices and rapidly shrinking horizons, I suddenly found myself at the centre of an expanding world where new opportunities were blossoming every day.

There was, however, a great deal of serious work to be done. Sobriety had pulled me to safety from the absolute brink of too late, and my life lay in smoking and devastated ruins around me. My flat was a disaster; years of chaotic partying and neglect had left it looking sordid and unloved. It wasn't just the physi-cal wreckage, though: the flat had become uninhabitable for me, a material manifestation of all my unhappiness. Too many grim memories, too many desperate days and painful nights had been spent there for me to ever again be able to think of it as a safe home.

My most terrible failing, though, was in my relationship with my son Joey. He was eight years old and had been living with my mother for around twelve months when I got sober. The shame that I had felt at being that most reviled of creatures, a mother who abandons her own child, had just become one more excuse to retreat into my alcohol-cushioned cell. With sobriety came horror, guilt and a fierce and urgent desire to repair the relationship with Joey, I hoped, before it was too late.

Nobody actually wants to be a bad parent. We all set out with high hopes not to make the same mistakes as our own parents and to raise our children as happy, healthy and secure people; yet sometimes it seems as though achieving this is the most difficult and unlikely thing in the world. There was a time when all that was required to be a good parent was to feed, clothe and house one's children, but family life is much more demanding now. Today we are expected to nurture self-esteem and build secure foundations for emotional health. The playground defiance of 'sticks and stones may break my bones, but names can never harm me' now seems curiously misguided, a ludicrous, topsy-turvy untruth. These days we know that broken bones will heal and damaged limbs can return to their former golden strength; but sharp words can bite into a soul, leaving wounds that sting and burn forever.

I was twenty-four when I gave birth to Joey. His father and I had met through a jazz and drinking club, and alcohol was one of the things that underpinned our relationship, right from our very first drunken date. We blundered into marriage and parenting with idiotically little thought or planning, and split up around the time of Joey's first birthday, having found, somewhat unsurprisingly, that our marriage had neither the strength nor substance to adapt to the demands of adult life. I was twenty-five years old, single again and, like most of my peers, looking forward to getting out and having fun after a couple of years of, as I saw it then, domestic misery. I don't think I ever gave a moment's thought to the fact that I was really pretty young to have already notched up a divorce and a baby – why would I? As the child of two serial divorcees myself, it was the only kind of family life I knew, and a situation I had always expected to find myself in. This was familiar ground for me, and somewhere I was comfortable. With no experience of a two-parent family, I could not begin to imagine how power and responsibility was shared. Certainly I had no reason to examine my own behaviour or choices, or to wonder if, perhaps, I was not embarking on the most fruitful path.

Over the next few years there were a lot of parties at my house, a lot of people and a lot of alcohol. And it was fun, or at least a good approximation of fun; if ever I noticed that the laughter was a little hollow, or the smiles a little manic, another drink would always smooth over any bumpy feelings. I was always the life and soul, revelling in my recklessness and proud of my partying stamina; the bad crowd that other people fell in with. I was a wild and reckless phase people went through, somewhere on the path to maturity.

From the very beginning Joey was affected by my drinking. He was never beaten or abused, nothing so blatantly problematic, but he could make his own breakfast at three years old. At a time when most kids are little more than babies, he was learning self-reliance. Sometimes there would be days when I was too hungover to get him to nursery, so he would have to spend the day at home in his pyjamas, trying not to irritate me. Then, as I veered into a dysfunctional relationship with another heavy drinker, Joey's needs were regularly placed second to my trying to cope with an increasingly chaotic life. A child's early years should be a time of feeling secure and unencumbered by responsibility but for Joey, who was already a self-contained little soul, it was just a time for him to learn that the world was an essentially unreliable and unfriendly place.

There are so many ways you can fail a child; they are so powerless, so dependent on you for everything, so ignorant of anything other than the truth you offer them. My crimes were largely of omission with Joey, but nevertheless it should be every child's right to have those carefree years. This is the time in their life when needs are magically met and safety envelops every breath. But I was barely mature enough to be able to look after myself; living up to the responsibilities of motherhood was clearly beyond me and so my child, as children often do, had to pay for my incompetence with his childhood.

Of course, I did love my son, and desperately so. I adored Joey and would sit by his bed for hours at night, watching him sleep, filled with love and wonder at his perfectness. At other times I would be seized with an irresistible urge to scoop him up and cover his little dark head with kisses, but that love just made the guilt more ferocious, until, by the end of my drinking, the simple act of holding my boy could cause me to weep shame-filled tears. Alcoholism is very often described as an illness these days and certainly, when I look back on the woman I was then, I see a sickness, a sadness and a seeming inability to find a way out of the horrible mess in which I was living. But I hesitate to call it a disease, with all the implications of helplessness and victimhood and the mitigation of responsibility. The truth is there was always a door out. In life we all make a thousand choices every day; I was just too blind or too stupid or too self-ish to see it.

As time went on and things, of course, got worse, it became harder and harder to ignore the fact that I was hurting my son. I felt like a monster. I was in a relationship with a man who abused me physically and emotionally, and I'd reached that point, like so many abused women, where I believed that this was all I was worth. My boyfriend never actually hurt Joey, but my son saw me with black eyes and broken noses and he was afraid for me. He learned that I was unreliable and inconsistent, that the house he lived in was dirty and chaotic, and often filled with strangers into the small hours. I fell into that desperate alcoholic spiral of drinking to escape the colossal guilt and vehement self-loathing that only grew bigger with every drink-fuelled day. Eventually his weekend visits to my mother's house grew into long weekends until, finally, he began to live with her full-time. I was very near to my lowest point by now, drinking around the clock, drinking in secret, wracked with guilt and shame that I was unable to care for my own child (although, in retrospect, it was clearly best for Joey to be away from me at that point). It had definitely stopped being fun. Alcoholism at its rock bottom is a sordid, painful, terrifying condition as well as a deeply selfish one. I could not stop for Joey's sake, I could not do anything for anyone. I could only feel self-pity, self-loathing, selfish.

The end, when it came, was unforeseen and immediate. Something cracked: survival instinct perhaps, or maybe I had just finally had enough. Whatever it was, I was too beaten to fight it and just the act of surrender brought an instantaneous and unexpected flood of glorious, blissful relief. By the end of my drinking, the sheer effort involved in simply trying to prevent the whole damaged show from collapsing about me was almost super-human. The daily lies, denials and half-arsed attempts to sweep up the worst of the exponentially growing debris was draining every last drop of life and spirit from me. So letting go, finally, and allowing the truth to wash unhindered across my world was actually quite exhilarating and ecstatic. Despite the physical pain of withdrawal, and the emotional turmoil it unleashed, this bubble of relief and release was still enough to buoy me through the difficult early days.

Early recovery is a truly bizarre adventure. When you are stripped of all your defences, shaking with DTs, sleepless and weepy, it is perhaps not the ideal time to start trying to repair a relationship with an understandably suspicious eight-year-old boy but, once the fog of alcohol was lifted and the full enormity of how I had betrayed my son began to hit me, I could think of nothing else. Of course, taking Joey back to the house that had been the scene of so much misery was out of the question, and so I joined my son in my mother's home, which seemed a fitting base from which to launch my second attempt at adulthood.

It is impossible to overstate the degree of guilt and shame I felt. Without a drink to hide behind, I was horrified by my actions and terrified that Joey had been damaged beyond repair. In those first months back together, I gently courted him, taking it slowly, not wanting to overwhelm him with my need to make everything OK. I'd been putting my own needs first for a very long time, and now it was time to step back and let him dictate the pace at which trust would grow. Fortunately nature was on my side; by and large children want to love their parents, and even in the most abusive home the child yearns, most often, for reconciliation rather than escape. Certainly this was true for Joey. Did I deserve his forgiveness? I don't know, but I do know that I was utterly grateful for it.

Five months into my sobriety, and just past the stage of shaking and sleeplessness, Joey and I moved into our new home. It was a wonderfully quirky, crooked little house on Carnaby Street, spiritual home of the Sixties and swinging London, and still a bustling, busy place in the heart of the West End. The house felt like a protector, safe for Joey and for me and, as spring kicked its way into London's streets, the sense of rebirth for both of us was palpable. New shoots of optimism were unfolding everywhere, tendrils of hope snaked delicately around each part of our new life and, for the first time in a long while, blossoms of laughter gave a cheerful, brash beauty to each day.

It is astounding how much life can change in just a few months. The grim hopelessness of the last days of my drinking felt foreign and far away. Joey was starting to relax and to actually trust that this new life was real, and I was energised and positive. My recovery programme had brought me into contact with spiritual ideas for the first time in my life and I found, to my great surprise, a resonance with the idea of a higher power. There is nothing more joyful than unbridled optimism; the absolute conviction that all problems, internal or external, can be fixed is as close to ecstasy as the human heart can get. I was evangelical about this new life; my gratitude at my eleventh-hour rescue was such that I felt duty bound to 'carry the message'. If I could do it, if someone so grubby and guilty could be given a second chance, then I was certain that it must be available to all, and that all would want it.

It was not all plain sailing though. The original demons that I had tried to drown with alcohol had been joined by plenty more over my drinking years, and now they were on the loose and desperate to bring me down. Painfully and painstakingly I unpicked the fabric of my life; smoothing and mending, cleaning, folding, gradually bringing order and harmony where there had been discord and disarray.

In recovery you have to learn to do everything differently. The way you think, act, feel all has to change. You learn a new perspective, turn yourself inside out, look, fix, mend, change; it is exhausting and, at times, painful but I worked hard at it and made progress quickly because, no matter how uncomfortable facing my demons became, nothing scared me more than going back to the hell I'd come from.

My relationship with Joey was not the only one that had been damaged. My family had been kept at arm's length for many years, as I tried to hide from them the awful reality of my life. I don't have a big family; I was the only child of a single mother for the first ten years of my life and she would call us 'the smallest family in the world'. Life was presented to me as an adventure that we had been thrown into together. I grew up fast, a serious, studious child in a world full of immature adults. As a child of the flower-children, I was steeped in the beliefs and attitudes of the hippy generation, who really did believe, bless them, that they were going to make the world a more beautiful place. So I learned that the world was divided into two types of people: there were people 'like us' who were bohemian, unconventional, hedonistic, love-creating and, most importantly, right. Then there were people who were 'square'; unimaginative, self-confined, rat-racing, experience-hating, often bigoted and most definitely wrong. The world was very black and white (or, rather, grey and rainbow-hued) and drugs were considered an important tool in unlocking the secrets of a happy and harmonious life.

My relationship with my mother is as complex and multi-faceted as most mother-daughter relationships, and my years of drinking and self-abuse had strained it to breaking point on a number of occasions. Now though, to my mother's credit and my eternal gratitude, she was ready to leave past battles and judgements behind and throw her considerable support and resources into helping me get back on my feet. Without her unflinching love and help it is highly likely that Joey and I would both have sustained considerably more long-term damage than we did. Despite the heartache I must have caused over the years, when the chips were down she was there all the way.

My family is big on loyalty, we stick together whatever, and I have learned to value this quality above almost anything. Of course, there have been times when our unwavering insistence on unswerving loyalty has brought its own problems. Conflicts of interest between friends and family have probably affected all of us at times, and there have been some painful and ugly family rows over it but, on balance, I still think that blind loyalty is probably a good thing in a family – at least you know where you are with it.

My brother Charlie was born, the product of my mother's brief second marriage, when I was ten and I adored him from the first day. The huge age gap meant that we were spared the usual sibling flashpoints of competition and envy. My relationship with my brother was always close and moved through the stages of nursemaid, then playmate, mentor and finally, by the time he reached sixteen, friends. We were also comrades. After years of surviving the insanity of our bohemian family life alone, I finally had an ally who could laugh with me at the absurdities of what passed for normal in our house, and back me in the increasingly frequent clashes with my mother. Despite the closeness between Charlie and me, and despite the common ground we share, we remain very different people. In some ways my brother is like a better version of me, the modified model where all the most glaring faults have been ironed out. Where I am reckless, Charlie is cautious; where I positively ooze taciturn anti-socialness, he is the ultimate 'people person'. Charlie has always been popular; his beautiful spirit and generous heart draw people to him, and his friends would do anything for him. He knows *everybody*. Truly, it's extraordinary; from rock stars to gangsters he simply cannot help but make friends. His first sentence was 'what's your name?' which he would chant from his pushchair, pointing at interesting-looking passers-by, as I, awkwardly gawky and prepubescent, trundled his buggy through the streets around our home.

My mother's third and current husband is Pierre, who has been at her side for thirty years now. They are business partners as well as husband and wife, having owned a succession of restaurants together over the years. Pierre was eighteen years old and fresh from school when he met my mother. She was thirty-three with a just toddling baby and a fiercely protective twelve-year-old daughter. She also had a husband who was serving time in a French prison for smuggling cannabis. I was not delighted by Pierre's arrival on the scene; when my mum had married husband number two, shortly after having his baby, I had been given my first taste of a proper family life. Charlie's dad, Tony, had come as a package deal with pillar-of-society parents who lived in a beautiful thatched house in Hertfordshire. Spending time with them was like being dropped into the middle of an Enid Blyton novel, all scrummy cakes and village fêtes. After my wild roller-coaster childhood, I was utterly entranced by the normality of their world and I was thrilled to be a part of it. Tony's arrest had driven a bulldozer through this new-found stability; we had no idea how long he'd be gone, but we knew it might be a very long time indeed. I was heartbroken, but I wrote regular letters to the various prisons he was moved to, and I would go and stay with his parents when my mother made her fortnightly trips to visit him.

And then Pierre appeared on the scene. I'm sure my mother never meant to fall in love; Pierre was just a diversion for a short while, until her husband came home. But I was angry and upset and, with just six years between Pierre and me, we fought – as teenagers do. Of course, the months of Tony's incarceration turned into years; and by the time he was released he'd changed, she'd changed, life had moved on... It was all such a long time ago, but it took a while for my relationship with Pierre to recover from its bumpy and resentful start. Today it lies somewhere between friends and siblings; we still bicker occasionally, but that's family for you. In my times of crisis, Pierre has always offered low-key but unflinching support.

I have a father too, although you won't find a great deal about him in this book. It's not so much that there's any bad feeling between us, it's just that he's never been very evident in my life. My shotgun-wedded parents split up when I was just a few weeks old. My father, seventeen years of age when I was born, and clearly terrified of the wife and child he'd suddenly acquired, ran away to sea. He really did, he joined a ship and that became his life; it still is in fact. The sailor's life suited my dad; no responsibilities, no ties, a girl (or two) in every port, drinking and gambling around the world and a decent pay packet at the end of the month. What's not to love for a good-looking and high-spirited young man? He remained friends with my mother, despite his obvious unwillingness to shoulder his portion of the responsibility for my well-being; and he would pitch up every year or so, laden with gifts from around the world. A fur coat from Russia perhaps, a piece of modern Scandinavian jewellery bought in the shipboard shop, caviare for my mum (traded with Russian sailors for jeans and Marlboro) or, best of all, candy and T-shirts from America which would impress my schoolfriends.

There were a couple of holidays too. He took me to Cyprus, to visit the village where he was born and meet my great-grandfather. I was eight years old and I can still remember the comforting taste of coffee made with syrupy-sweet condensed milk that I was given. I can also remember my abject horror at the squealing of the pig whose throat was cut in celebration of our visit. The whole village turned out to share the wonderfully fresh pork, spit-roasted as the centrepiece of the celebrations. But I, a city child in every way, could not eat a single bite of an animal that I had watched die, even though my stomach ached with hunger and the delicious smell of crackling filled the air.

At thirteen my dad took me to Disney World while the ship he worked on was in dry dock in Florida. I can clearly remember being excited and overwhelmed by my first trip to America, but I cannot remember a single conversation with my father. And that's the thing: I don't know my dad. In over forty years our relationship has never moved beyond the superficial. We don't know each other and, I assume, now we never will. I don't think I've ever missed him. How can you miss that which you never had? But I do sometimes wonder whether I would have been different, had my father been a meaningful presence in my life.

My dad has two other children besides me, both younger than I am, and both from his second marriage. My brother Antony is the same age as Charlie, over ten years younger than me; and Katerina, my sister, is another eleven or so years younger than that. I have had small amounts of contact with Antony over the years, but Katerina has lived abroad for most of her life so I've seen much less of her. Our father never encouraged us to be close, or even friends, and, when you factor in the huge age gaps and the physical distances between us, it's easy to see why our relationships haven't exactly flourished. Now, somewhat belatedly, we are all trying to bridge the gaps between us and I am enjoying getting to know my younger siblings, and bringing them into my family life.

The intensity and closeness of our immediate familial relationships means that we have never really gone in for extended family in a big way. I used to think that all families were strange and dysfunctional, mine no more so than anyone's. Now, though, I've come to realise that mine really is odder than most, but I like to think that we carry our insanity lightly and with aplomb. There are, of course, aunts, uncles and cousins; the usual collection of relatives on both my mother's and father's sides but, with a few notable exceptions, they are far away both geographically and emotionally. Whenever I bring to mind family, I think of this tight little core who live in an area of just a couple of square miles and slip in and out of each other's consciousness several times each day.

So, as I started recovery, that was my family: Joey, Charlie, Pierre, my mother and me, and while it's safe to say I had a fair bit of bridge-building to do, it is also true that they made it easy for me. They became my support and my cheering section, and they took as much delight in my optimism and sense of achievement as I did myself.

In the light of what was to come, I am grateful for my idiosyncratic upbringing and unconventional relatives. When life has rarely thrown 'Normal' at you, you are much less likely to be derailed by a sudden swerve in the road. The only thing I ever expected in life was to be surprised; upheaval was as much a part of my growing up as scraped knees and penny ice-pops on sunny days. At just five years old I woke one morning to be told: 'Get in the car, we're moving to Italy.' And we did, there and then; driving over the Alps in a rickety motor with all our possessions tied to the roof, and a 'slot-in' record player next to me on the back seat.

So when the world turned upside down, I was ready for it. Or, rather, I wasn't *not* ready. A lifetime's training meant that my psyche clicked automatically into crisis mode. I may be unreliable, chaotic, flaky even... But when you're backed up against the wall, you really want to have me in your corner.

It all fits together now, and the big picture just keeps on getting bigger.

~ 3 ~

I've never been a very good judge of men. That's another of the problems that comes from living in a bubble of alcohol: vodka does tend to cloud your judgement somewhat. My relationship history resembled a rather bloody farce and was yet another manifestation of the chaos that I managed to attract. I can spot Mr Wrong a mile off and, of course, even in a room full of love-struck Prince Charmings hanging on my every word, I will be drawn to the one man who looks at me with disdain and who can intuitively see exactly how to undermine my confidence and drive me to frustration and despair. It doesn't take a genius to work out that I have been a woman who has 'issues' with men; nor is it, I guess, too great a leap of imagination to see that this *might* have something to do with my notably absent father. However, this is not about blame and, to be quite honest, whatever mistakes my parents made, they were mere stepping stones en route to the huge, momentous and life-threatening errors I managed to make all by myself.

There have been some good guys of course, one or two, but none of them managed to maintain my interest for any length of time. My first husband, Joey's father, is a fundamentally decent man who happened to be in the wrong place at the right time. We were hopeless as a married couple but I couldn't wish for a nicer ex and now, some seventeen years after our divorce, and with both of us settled and happily remarried, our relationship is probably the best it's ever been. In the main though, it's hard to have much respect for someone who treats you well when you're filled with self-loathing; so the good guys never stood much of a chance with me.

The men might have been grim, but at least there were plenty of them. The restless search for *something* had me bouncing my ping-pong path from bastard to bastard and this, combined with a fatal attraction to danger and an unhealthy appetite for risk-taking, was the perfect way for me to feed every festering insecurity and bitter drop of self-doubt. My last serious relationship before stopping drinking was a five-year epic war with a man who was, unlikely though it seems, every bit as damaged as me. Five long, ugly years of trauma and drama, full of anger, fear and pain. It goes without saying that only someone with the lowest self-esteem would put themselves into such a god-awful relationship and, indeed, by the end of our time together the only thing we still had in common was that we both hated me.

Giving up booze and giving up boys, for me, went hand in hand. It may be a terrible cliché to say that I needed to develop a healthy relationship with myself before I could manage to be with anyone else, but it is the simple truth. On entering recovery you are 'strongly advised' that you should try to get a year's sobriety under your belt before embarking on a relationship and for me, who had never been single for more than a few days at a time, this was a terrifying prospect.

What was even more terrifying was the thought of remaining stuck in the grim pit that described the final days of my drinking. The idea that I might be trapped forever in the horrible misery that had become my life was so awful I was prepared even to face my terrible fear of being alone and 'work the programme' to the best of my ability. My strategy for staying man-free (one day at a time) was idiotically simple: I made sure I didn't meet any. What this actually meant was that I attended meetings that were almost exclusively attended by gay men. I didn't know that I could trust myself anywhere else; far easier to just remove the temptation in the same way as an alcoholic tries to avoid the pub. Eventually, after several months of celibacy, I stopped thinking of myself primarily as an 'available' woman; stopped giving out the subtle, subconscious signals that invite amorous attention, and started to feel comfortable with my new status. This was a whole new world for me; independent, self-sufficient, unafraid. My relationship with Joey blossomed and I began to understand that I didn't need a man to complete me: I was enough for myself; I was alone and it was OK. Most extraordinary of all, I began to like myself.

I don't think that I was particularly unusual in imagining that having a man by my side was an essential prerequisite for happiness; even here in the twenty-first century, a lot of women calculate their own value according to how much they are valued by men. It's a sad fact that, very often, the only reflection we truly believe in is the one we see in a man's eyes. Learning to adjust my perspective, to see how much I could mean to *myself*, and all the power and pride that brought, was a revelation. I didn't need to be afraid of loneliness, I didn't need to accept abuse, I didn't have to be trapped; things that seem obvious to most people but were news to me. I felt reborn: this extraordinary sense of self, of possibility and of completeness was overwhelming and wonderful. For the first time in my life I looked ahead to an unknown future with optimism and free from fear. And in my heart I knew, without a shadow of doubt, that even if I were never to meet a man I could love again, everything would still be fine.

It's funny how things work out. Sometimes it seems as though life is just a series of elaborate hoops through which we must jump in the right way, and in the right order. God's great game, where we collect tokens of wisdom or experience that gain us entry to the next level. Certainly in my case, when I had finally learned that I *really* didn't need a man, when I had reached the point of contented self-sufficiency, that was the exact moment that love walked into my world.

I can remember with absolute clarity the first time I saw Danny. It was mid-summer, a glorious, sunshiny day, and I was in a blissfully light-hearted mood. Almost a year sober, I was the secretary of an AA meeting in the basement of a Soho church. The meeting room was windowless and gloomy, a stark contrast to the streaming brightness of the street outside, and the meeting itself was solemn and hushed, despite the fact that it was well attended to the point of being crowded. I suppose there were about forty people there; every chair was filled and there were even people perched on top of a row of tables at the back.

Danny arrived late. I had already started the meeting and he tried to slip in unnoticed, not wanting to interrupt the flow of the weekly speaker. I saw him squeeze himself on to the end of one of the tables and was immediately struck by his fragile beauty. He was only a couple of months clean, still in rehab in fact, and skinny as a stick. His hair was peroxide blonde and spiky and he had the bluest eyes I'd ever seen, obvious even from the other side of the room. And he shone. He lit up the room as though he had brought a part of the sun-drenched day into the subterranean gloom.

I was entranced by this delicate flower of a boy although, at this point, my thoughts were not consciously romantic. For one thing, Danny looked much younger than he really was and I judged his age to be nineteen or so – far too young for me. And then, having surrounded myself with gay men for so long, I automatically assumed that a young and incredibly pretty boy could not possibly be straight. The final antidote to any lustful thoughts was that he was still in his very early days of sobriety, any approach I made would be considered unacceptably predatory. For all these reasons, despite how powerfully I was drawn to him, I simply didn't see Danny as boyfriend material, not even a tiny bit.

We became friends, hanging out after meetings, discussing our recovery and how we'd got there. The beauty of friendships formed in recovery is you wear your imperfections on your sleeve. No one ends up in AA without a murky story behind them, and there's a certain peace of mind that comes from knowing that your darkest traits and grimmest skeletons are already public knowledge and accepted. Honesty is the very best basis for any relationship and, in actual fact, the absence of romantic feelings between Danny and me in the early days of our relationship enhanced this level of openness and easy friendship.

I know the exact point where our hearts made the jump from friends to lovers. We had been somewhere, I don't exactly remember where, and had journeyed back into town together. We said goodbye at a crowded street corner and kissed each other, a friendly kiss, on the cheek. I walked away and, after a few steps, turned to look and wave again and Danny was still standing on the corner, watching me walk away and smiling at me. Our eyes met and suddenly I knew. It was so obvious, so glaringly, blindingly clear that we would be together, and we both knew it.

Everything about the beginning of our relationship was wonder-filled and as different from any of my other relationships as it was possible to be. With Danny everything was easy and natural and right. There was passion, of course, but even this was tender and uplifting rather than the stomach-churning roller-coaster rides of my previous affairs. With Danny the sense of homecoming and of connection was profound; I think we both were filled with an overwhelming sense of relief at having found each other. And there was never the tiniest scrap of doubt, for either of us, that we had met our life's match.

Of course, nothing is ever quite that simple. Danny and I may have known that we were meant to be together, but it was not a notion that was going to be shared by everyone. You see Danny, my new-found soulmate, was Jewish. In fact, to be exact, he is the eldest son of an orthodox Jewish rabbi and had grown up, kosher and practising, in the heart of the Jewish community. I, in complete contrast, had grown up in a cheerfully agnostic environment. My hippy-dippy mother ruled nothing out except dogma; so to call my spiritual upbringing wishy-washy would be to imbue it with a gravitas it really didn't deserve.

Coming from a home where religious beliefs were considered to be of so little importance, it was almost impossible for me to understand why my non-Jewishness was such a big issue for Danny. I had no idea that, in the modern western world, families could still be divided over such matters; and though Danny tried to explain to me why he felt unable to tell his parents about our relationship, I still found it odd. Surely, I reasoned, once they met me, once they saw how very 'right' we were together, saw their son's happiness, they would accept me into their hearts and their family?

Eventually Danny realised that he really had to tell them about me; it was clear that our relationship was serious and very likely permanent. He drove the hundred miles or so to the town where they lived, ready to come clean about his shiksa girlfriend but, alas, nerves overcame him in the end and after a tension-filled day with his father, he drove back to London without having told him anything. He did manage to break the awful news to his mother who, quite rightly, refused to be her son's messenger and tell her husband. I think that she had probably guessed that we were more than just good friends. A mother knows these things, and perhaps even Rabbi Shisler had a tiny inkling, but I'm sure she hoped that I would be a passing fling before the serious search for a wife began. Now, however, she could no longer pretend that this relationship would quickly fizzle out and, to her eternal credit, she swallowed her disappointment and all her hopes for her eldest son, and reluctantly accepted me because I made him happy.

Despite this fear of his parents' reaction we continued to develop our relationship and look towards a future together; and the most natural consequence of our growing commitment was the desire to have a child. I was thirty-four already with a ten-year-old son, so I didn't particularly want to wait around. Danny, although eight years younger than me, also felt ready to start a family and so, just three months into our relationship, we threw our little remaining caution to the wind and set about trying to get me pregnant.

Now, I am well aware that this seems beyond foolhardy. Certainly if a woman came to me and said, 'I've just started a relationship with some guy who's pretty young, not long out of rehab, doesn't have a proper job or any money and he can't tell his family about me...*and we're gonna have a baby*,' I would be advising caution and common sense and, like most sane people, urging her to stop being so reckless. I know all the reasons why you shouldn't leap into parenthood with someone you hardly know and I can tell you all the terrible things that could happen to you, let alone the awful damage you could inflict on your child. But somehow, even knowing all that, none of it mattered. I asked Danny if he was absolutely sure he wanted to have a child with me and I remember him saying that he had never been so sure of anything in his life. We just knew. There were no bells ringing, no corks popping, no fanfares; just an overwhelming sense of rightness. I don't know how else to explain our apparent insanity, but no one around us, none of the people who were close to us, who knew our lives and our relationship, thought we were crazy or deluded. And so, with eyes and hearts wide open, we jumped.

* * *

I got up extra early to do the test, with the kit bought secretly the day before. I was sitting on the bathroom floor, watching the little blue line appear and trembling with excitement and awe. Danny was still sleeping as I slipped back into bed. I whispered our news into his ear and he responded by drawing me into a hug, smiling in his still half-sleeping state, making me feel safe, happy and loved. We were really going to be a family.

* * *

The reality of having a baby on the way did rather force Danny's hand when it came to telling his parents. It was *just* conceivable that he could keep a girlfriend under wraps, but a first grandchild? In the end he broke the news by letter; it seemed the best way of imparting the information calmly and clearly. The response also came in a letter. Danny's father wrote simply setting out the fact that he would be unable to acknowledge either me or any non-Jewish grandchild. The letter was not cruel but it was unequivocal: whilst Danny would always be loved and welcomed into his parents' home, his family would never be entertained. Not in a physical sense, not even as a topic of conversation; we simply could not exist in the world he came from.

I was shocked. Despite the fact that Danny had told me precisely what would happen and how his father would respond, when the letter actually came it stunned me. I suppose I had assumed that a child would somehow breach the walls of Jewish laws and traditions; at this point I still didn't really understand such thinking and I was, of course, completely unfamiliar with Jewish culture. But, Danny assured me, this was to be expected and in actual fact his father's reaction, with his desire to maintain a relationship with his son, would be considered unacceptably liberal in some quarters. Some families, he told me, would sit shiva, the formal period of mourning after a Jewish funeral, for the errant son, telling the world symbolically that he had died. More to the point, I could see that Danny not only understood his father's decision, but he also respected him for his integrity and utter absence of hypocrisy and so, bewildering as it was to me, I vowed to do the same. I may not be able to understand, I reasoned, but that didn't mean it didn't make sense. I couldn't understand Serbo-Croat either, but that didn't make me think it wasn't a real language.

The letter from Danny's father also made it quite clear that Danny's mother, Anne, would be making her own decision over contact with us and our new baby. The rabbi was careful to make sure we knew that he spoke for himself alone, and would not be imposing his decision on the rest of the family. Danny's mother was not about to be denied her first grandchild; she came to see us and said, through tears, that she would do whatever she could to support us. I think this time must have been unbelievably difficult for the Shislers. Family is such a central element of Jewish culture: it is the home, rather than the synagogue, that provides the focus for much of a Jew's spiritual life. A first grandchild would, under normal circumstances, be an occasion for much celebration and joy, but this child would be unheralded, a dark secret that most of the family would never meet or even hear about. It was a heart-breaking situation, for Danny as well as for his parents, and all I could do was watch and pray and trust that somehow we would work it all out.

Danny's siblings were the next to know. Simon, his younger brother by two years, accepted me immediately and unequivocally. The boys were close and hugely supportive of each other, so Simon's happiness at our joy was genuine and greatly appreciated. Danny's younger sister, Abi, was taking a gap year in Israel and Danny was less certain about her reaction. The age gap was bigger, seven years, and Abi was by far the most religiously inclined of the three Shisler children. When I finally got to meet her, several months into my pregnancy, she was certainly wary but she also made it clear that she would support her brother and his new family. I think that Abi was the one who felt the most torn by the situation. She was distressed for her parents and also foresaw logistical problems for Danny, having to hide his life at the inevitable family weddings, birthdays and religious festivals.

In my heart of hearts I suppose I had always assumed that, once the baby was born, Danny's father would soften but, as I got to know Simon and Abi, it became abundantly clear that Danny had in no way exaggerated the situation: we would never be accepted. I worried that Danny would regret his drastic step into a life with me, but he never wavered, not for a moment; and if he ever felt a twinge of regret at letting go of his Jewish community, he certainly never showed it to me.

There were other family members who we told, just a few; and by and large they were supportive and happy for us, although saddened by the inevitable estrangement of father and son. It was a difficult situation for everyone; nevertheless those who did meet me were kind and congratulatory, for which I was very grateful. Again and again, family members sought to reassure me that I must not take this personally. It didn't matter how nice I was or that I was a good person, the only significant issue was my non-Jewishness.

Aside from the insoluble Jewish problem, life, love and my belly were blooming. My family were unequivocally delighted by my pregnancy and drew Danny into their hearts without reservation. As for Danny, it turned out that the charming but penniless young man I had fallen in love with was hiding some seriously marketable skills. Back on the job market he was making astounding professional progress as a software developer. It suddenly became clear that we were going to have real financial security; an absolutely unexpected bonus, and we started looking around for a house to buy.

My pregnancy was fairly textbook and unremarkable. I'm not a particularly good pregnant person; I get lousy morning sickness and a million niggling irritants from backache to constipation, which I huff and sigh about around the clock. Despite the little discomforts and my endless whining about them, I did actually enjoy my pregnancy. We discovered at an early ultrasound that I was carrying a baby girl and we decided to name her Eve Amber. I don't really understand people who don't want to know the sex of their baby because they 'don't want to spoil the surprise'. As if meeting your baby for the first time is not exciting and surprising enough already! Do they imagine that those of us who want to know at the earliest moment look back on the birth saying 'well it was a bit of an anticlimax really, because we already knew it was a girl/boy' as though a baby was like the Christmas present under your mother's bed that you'd sneaked a peek at. Personally I like to know so I can plan names and outfits, and break up the interminable nine-month wait.

My mother and I made the most of the shopping opportunities that a pregnancy provides and from around the fourth month were cooing over little dresses and teeny-tiny socks in Baby Gap and road-testing prams at full speed through the aisles of John Lewis, before collapsing in fits of giggles, much to the bemusement of the shop assistants. I had one of those neat little baby bumps that meant I barely needed maternity clothes and was able to look presentable and pulled-together right through to the end. Because Joey's birth had been an emergency Caesarean, it seemed sensible to go for a c-section this time too. This time though, being elective, I could book in for it at thirty-eight weeks and have it under local anaesthetic with Danny present the whole time.

It was exciting, and miraculous. Danny was already a fantastic stepfather to Joey and I was longing to see him as a father, holding his own baby. I felt lucky, truly blessed, to be in this situation. Having come from such a dark place, having made so many mistakes in my past, to be given this second chance felt like a divine gift. After years of chaos, fear and pain I was happy and settled, with a wonderful man who loved me, a repaired relationship with my adored son, a daughter on the way and a bright and financially secure future ahead of me. Each day brought new reasons to pinch myself and make sure that this was not an incredible dream. For Danny too, the contrast between his life with me and the awfulness of his pre-rehab days was profound; even Joey was buzzing with the relief that comes from having survived a disaster. And we were all counting the days until baby Eve made her appearance.

I was to be admitted to hospital the night before my Caesarean section, so they could make all the final health checks and supervise my adherence to the pre-operative nil-by-mouth rule. Danny and I went for our last baby-free dinner at a local Greek restaurant and then we walked to the hospital. It seemed strange to have to say goodnight but, by this point, I think we were too excited to even chat to each other; it was almost a relief when Danny left me and went home, and I could sit and allow my happy, busy thoughts to wander. The nurses brought me a sleeping pill, clearly very experienced with over-anxious and over-excited mothers-to-be and, eventually, my consciousness switched off for a few hours, although I'm not sure that you could really call it sleep. The next morning Danny was taken out for a 'last non-parental breakfast' by his brother Simon, and then brought to the hospital. Danny was in excellent spirits but poor Simon seemed to be carrying all his anxiety for him. He was jumpy and nervous but eventually left us alone and retired to somewhere nearby where he would sit, chain-smoking and glued to his mobile phone, waiting for news of the baby.

Joey had been born under general anaesthetic, so I had no idea what to expect for the birth. Eventually Danny and I were gowned up, me in the ludicrous, bottom-revealing surgical robe and support stockings, Danny in surgical scrubs with dinky paper hat, and we were taken down to theatre. The surgeons and anaesthetist introduced themselves and before I knew it I was numb from the chest down and lying on a table with a screen separating my head from my belly. Danny was under strict instructions to stay on the head side of the screen. Even from the love of my life, some things are meant to stay private and I count my internal organs in this category.

Having a child by c-section is an extraordinary experience. Firstly, there's the way it feels: it's not painful, not at all, the epidural takes care of that, but that doesn't mean you can't feel it. It's a bizarre sensation, having someone rummaging around in your body, rather like they've dropped a coin between the cushions of a sofa and are trying to reclaim it. And the baby doesn't necessarily slip out very easily; in my case there was some serious tugging involved that actually saw me pulled down the table and almost right under the screen. I remember giggling at the absurdity and then, all of a sudden, she was out! The surgeon held her up above the screen and I saw a tiny red foot and then she was gone, to be cleaned and checked and weighed. Moments later our beautiful daughter was in our arms and I was shaking and crying with joy and relief that she was here and safe and so very, very beautiful.

Now, as I have never had a 'natural childbirth' I realise that I am not really in a position to compare but I do know that Evie's birth could not have been any more beautiful, emotional or moving. Those first few minutes holding our baby were as heart-stoppingly ecstatic as is humanly possible and it saddens me that so many women feel like failures if they don't manage to push the baby out themselves. It sometimes feels like women are being told that the purpose of pregnancy is to have a 'birth experience', rather than a baby.

Joey was the first to hear of Evie's birth, and then the rest of the calls were made. My family rushed to the hospital to meet our little girl; Simon and Abi were also desperate to meet their new niece, turning up within hours of her arrival. Danny's mother and grandmother, Booba Pauline, came too and there was no denying their love and commitment to the baby. I'm sure it was a bittersweet day for them, caught in this terrible wasteland between secrecy and pride, but I was too happy and too besotted with my perfect family to feel anything other than delight.

That night, when everyone had gone, I took her into the bed with me. Too emotional to sleep, I gazed at her perfect little face, said my thankful prayers and wept tears of gratitude and joy while my angelic daughter slept contentedly in my arms. Nature is a wonderful thing, it always gives us the child that is a perfect fit. I remember when Joey was born, I would actually feel pity for people who had daughters. I was the mother of A Son. And my son, my beautiful *boy* was, to me, the epitome of perfection. How awful, I reasoned, to be denied the chance to raise and love one of these miraculous creatures. But now, as I gazed on the tiny girl in my arms, I remembered an old saying: '*A son is your son till he takes him a wife; but a daughter's your daughter for the rest of your life.*' I was the mother of a girl, a daughter, I was truly blessed.

Having Evie really was just an unmitigated joy; everything about her was happy and uplifting. There were none of the anxieties that come with a first baby (at least, not for me – Danny, on the other hand, was as flustered and unsettled as any first-time father) and I was able to relax into mothering her right from the start. And she was so very *alive*. With Joey, I had, like most new mothers, listened to his every breath at night, praying that he would not somehow slip away from life. But Evie never caused me a moment's worry; she was tiny but feisty-strong and so clearly here to stay. She took to breastfeeding like a charm and gained weight in a perfect copy of the median line of the growth chart; by eight weeks she was sleeping through the night. Milestones were hit squarely and on time; she really was a dream baby.

When we found our perfect house, just a few weeks after her birth, it really felt that life couldn't get much better. Danny's career was going from strength to strength, Joey was happily settled into his new school and I was finding motherhood the second time around a breeze. I was completely smitten with Evie and determined to keep her at home with me for as long as possible. Joey had, out of necessity, gone to nursery from two years old, but I didn't want that again. One thing about having a big age gap between your kids is that you are really super-aware of how quickly their childhood slips away. This time I wanted to savour every moment of it.

We moved into the new house and immediately started work on it. We wanted an extra bathroom, a wall knocked down; it was going to be chaos for a while but, we reasoned, it would be well worth it to have the house just the way we wanted it. We were, I suppose, much like any other young family, filled with ideas, plans and optimism. I had the house decorated in rainbow bright colours – a sunshine yellow hallway, fuchsia for the kitchen and a bluebell sitting room; I wanted the house to look as uplifted as we felt. In truth, I suspect we were a little smug; certainly we thought we'd got this life lark well and truly nailed. Happiness? It just wasn't that hard, we reasoned. There was little that couldn't be fixed with the right attitude and a lick of multi-coloured paint. Having snatched our united victory from the absolute jaws of our individual defeats, we were certainly a little cocky, but our happiness and hopefulness were genuine and life was a lot of fun.

Shortly after moving into our new house, I was woken in the middle of the night by an urgent need to pee. Half asleep, I stumbled into the bathroom and sat on the toilet. And then, suddenly, I was wide awake as a realisation pierced my consciousness. I knew this feeling. The suddenly-weak bladder? A dull aching in my breasts? It hit me with the force of a bullet: I was pregnant again.

~ 4 ~

If only we could make life stand still. If we could freeze time at the moment when the sun was shining upon our face and the wind was at our back, how much simpler things would be. But, of course, as those irritating books of 'uplifting' thoughts always remind us, life is a journey, not a destination, and the only thing we can be sure of is that everything changes.

I didn't want to say anything to Danny until I was sure I was really pregnant; after all, it's easy to imagine things in the small hours when half asleep. Evie was only a few months old, I was still breastfeeding her, and my periods had not restarted since her birth, which meant that I couldn't even use that as an indication of pregnancy. The morning after my middle-of-the-night revelation I bought a testing kit and locked myself in the bathroom. The blue line appeared in the 'pregnant' window astonishingly quickly. There could be absolutely no doubt, another baby was on the way.

I called Danny who was delighted, excited and reassuring. My own feelings were more equivocal; still deeply immersed in the self-contained love affair of a mother and her newborn, I was not yet ready to open my heart to another child. Experience had taught me, however, that by the time the baby arrived I would be more than prepared and willing to meet him or her and I hung on to that thought, placing my faith in the instinctive ability of my heart to adapt to the new addition.

The maternity hospital's booking-in clinic sent me for an ultrasound scan immediately. The absence of any periods since before my last pregnancy meant that I had no way of knowing how far along I was, so a scan was the quickest way of finding out when the baby was due.

Evie slept peacefully in her pram, snuggled into her blanket, tiny thumb firmly planted in her little rosebud mouth, so beautiful. I winced as the ultrasound technician rolled the scanner over my full-to-bursting bladder, trying to find a good view of the still-minute being. 'It must be very early in the pregnancy,' she told me. 'The embryo is barely visible.' That surprised me. The speed and strength of the positive pregnancy test, combined with my ferocious morning sickness, had convinced me that the pregnancy was well established, so to hear that it was only just at the detectable stage was confusing. After a few more minutes of scanning and prodding my poor beleaguered bladder, she decided that she needed a better look than she was able to get with the present equipment. I was sent to pee while she prepared to give me a much more accurate internal ultrasound examination. Coming back into the room, much relieved, I found that there were now two technicians waiting by the monitor.

'I just wanted my colleague to check something for me,' said the sonographer. 'I hope you don't mind.' That probably should have alerted me to the fact that my scan was not normal but, in my pregnant air-headed state, nothing registered at all.

They both huddled around the screen as I lay on the examination table, nonplussed. I looked at the monitor: just about visible was a little pulsating spot – my new baby's heartbeat. Then the scanner was moved a tiny bit and suddenly, right there on the screen, another pulse. Another pulse, another tiny heartbeat. Twins!

Of course, *now* it made sense: the emphatic pregnancy test, the outrageous morning sickness, the endless trips to the loo. It wasn't that the pregnancy was very far advanced, it was the double dose of hormones being pumped into my system that accounted for my super-pregnant state. Oh crap.

I left the hospital in a daze, struggling to digest all the implications that would come from having three babies in a year. I called Danny at work and shakily gave him the news. He, hearing the rising panic in my voice, said he would come straight home to look after me. Then I phoned my mother. By coincidence she was out shopping with my father, on one of his infrequent visits to London, when I called her on her mobile phone. I could hear the screams of laughter and excitement from them both as I imparted my extraordinary news and despite my undoubted terror, even I could see that there was something quite comical in the seismic shift in my situation. It seemed just moments earlier I'd been a struggling, alcoholic, single parent of an only child and now, seemingly overnight, I was a thoroughly domesticated housewife and soon-to-be mother of *four*.

The news almost killed my brother Charlie, literally. I managed to call his mobile phone as he was in the middle of crossing a busy road and the resultant shock actually stopped him dead in his tracks, almost sending him under the wheels of an oncoming truck in the process.

My own feelings remained at the negative end of the scale. There was undoubtedly some kudos and excitement from the whole twin thing, but the glory felt like small compensation for having my neat and perfect life so comprehensively trashed. I was furious with these two little interlopers, thrusting their uninvited way into my family, stealing my time and strength from my poor little daughter. Now she would get only the barest whisper of maternal focus to herself, before the demands of two more babies drowned out the needs of her peaceful little soul. They were ganging up on her; it was all so unjust. And even though I managed to smile and nod when the inevitable congratulations flooded in from friends and family, inside I was raging with anger, disappointment and fear. The hospital had an ante-natal counsellor who, as it turned out, was unable to allay my fears, despite the fact that soothing pregnant women was, presumably, her main duty. In between bouts of violent morning sickness I knew I was slipping into depression; clearly I was going to have to find a way of coping with this new situation, or I would never make it through the pregnancy with my sanity intact.

It was Danny who found the solution in the end and he found it in a place I would never have thought to look: on the internet. It seems bizarre now: after all this was not very long ago – 1998; but the large-scale use of email outside academia or industry was only just starting to take off. I was certainly far from unusual in not having a personal email address, few people did, and the idea of internet communities was really quite alien to me, but that was about to change. Danny introduced me to the concept of an email list group; this was a simple way for groups of people with common interests to share information. The way it works is that the host computer holds a list of the email addresses of all the group's members. Any email (or 'post') sent to the list address is automatically distributed to all the members of the group. If people want to reply they can either email the individual who wrote the original post, thereby replying privately or, by replying to the list address, they can send their thoughts to the whole group. In this way it becomes easy to ask questions of a large group of subscribers, and to take part in detailed discussions between any number of people. These groups exist for almost any topic you can imagine. There are professional groups sharing technical information; disability groups pooling medical knowledge; groups offering support after bereavement; collectors; hobbyists; fandom... Every issue of human interest is there, and the one that Danny had found for me was for parents of twins.

Writing is, for me, an automatic response to times of stress and, in addition to this, I'd had a couple of years of twelve-step recovery where I'd learned to share my most intimate thoughts and feelings with roomfuls of strangers, so this was the perfect way for me to voice my fears. Most importantly, I could remain anonymous; it is the anonymity of AA meetings that allows such freedom and now I had found a parallel on the internet. There was no fear of being judged, nobody would even know who I was; I could open my heart with impunity.

That night I poured all the weight in my soul out into the ether. I wrote of my love for my daughter; my fear that her babyhood was being stolen by these two little gooseberries; I wrote about my resentment because our beautiful new home, that we had occupied for barely a couple of months, was already too small for our rapidly growing family. Then there were the other, more prosaic fears: how would my body cope with the pregnancy, just how big was I going to get? What would I do with three non-walkers; did they even make triple-pushchairs? How many nappies would I be changing? Mainly though, I just needed to acknowledge how out of control I felt. I knew that my life was going to change immeasurably and I wasn't ready. After all the sheer bloody, back-breaking effort I had made to knock myself and my world into decent shape, it was slipping through my fingers before I'd even had time to enjoy the achievement. It was slipping away and I couldn't stop it; this huge juggernaut of change was rattling towards me and I wanted to weep with frustration and rage.

It was cathartic, just the act of writing, of finding a space to be heard, helped. And having offloaded some of the anxiety and tension I'd been carrying, I slept a little easier that night; a little less burdened.

I'm not sure what I expected when I switched on my computer the following morning, but I was absolutely astounded by the outpouring of support I found. There were dozens of letters from mothers of twins, all sharing their own stories of fear and adjustment. These women understood my anxiety, and even my anger, and they told me that it didn't make me a bad person, it made me normal. Even women who had conceived twins only after long, emotionally draining fertility treatments were telling me that they had experienced doubts and worries. Women who had dreamed of holding a baby, who had pictured their perfect infant so many times, still found themselves perversely upset when they were told that there was an extra little person on the way, and that their cherished vision of motherhood would have to change. Letter after letter described the exact battle raging in both my head and my heart; I was clearly far from alone, and very far from being a monster. More importantly, though, the letters were reassuring. Again and again I read that, by the end of the pregnancy, these doubts had miraculously melted away and, without exception, the twins had come to be seen as the miraculous blessing they obviously were. Having twins was something truly special; I was now part of an elite group of mothers of multiples, and I would experience aspects of parenting I had never imagined. Even my biggest worry, my fear for poor little overshadowed Evie, was addressed. Of course, they told me, there would be less individual attention for my sweet girl, but her life would be immeasurably enriched by having two little playmates so close to her age. It was admittedly a huge difference from the eleven-year space between children that was all I had known, but I was starting to see that a family of similar-sized children just might have its advantages too.

I can't say that all my doubts and concerns miraculously and instantaneously dissolved, but I was greatly soothed, both by the reassurance that my heart would eventually learn to encompass the babies, but also by knowing that I had a place to turn to for been-there-done-that advice on the complexity of juggling children. Over the next few years, the Twins List community would become an important part of my life and writing to the group a near-daily activity. But, for now, it was enough that out-and-out panic had been averted. With the edge taken off my terror, I was finally able to turn my attention to the other major event on my horizon: Danny and I were getting married.

Of course, nothing in my life is ever simple and our wedding was no exception. We had already delayed it until after Evie's birth because I didn't want to walk up the aisle pregnant. Little did we think that by the time we'd organised everything, ironically enough, I would be pregnant again anyway – doubly so. We wanted to have a ceremony that was faith-based, no quick trip to the register office for us, and spiritually meaningful for us both. Obviously we couldn't marry in a synagogue and Danny still felt uncomfortable with overt symbols of Christianity, so the challenge was always going to be finding a location for the service. Finally we found a beautiful, leafy Unitarian chapel that was perfect. The Unitarians are probably the most non-dogmatic and inclusive religion you can find anywhere, and they were very experienced in performing mixed-faith weddings. We were encouraged to write our own vows and design our own service. Danny wanted to have elements of his Judaism incorporated into the ceremony so we chose a traditional Jewish chuppa, the canopy that the bride and groom stand beneath, for the centre-piece of the service, and we also included Hebrew readings of Jewish wedding prayers.

My brother Charlie was, at the time, sharing a flat with a bona fide pop star, who offered to sing for us in the chapel. Another friend, who was a florist, would decorate the chuppa and do my bouquet, and my mother's restaurant, then playing host to a top French chef, would do our reception. Car hire, dress fittings, invitations, everything came together beautifully; it was hard not to feel that the heavens were smiling upon our union.

The warm glow of approval that surrounded us had, of course, its limitations. Danny's brother Simon had agreed to be his best man and was as supportive as we could have wished, but he was the only member of Danny's family who promised to come to the wedding. My heart ached for Danny, marrying without his family there to celebrate with him but, by this time, I had learned not to be surprised by their distance. In any case, we were so very in love, so joyful about being together, that even this couldn't take the shine off our day or dim our perpetually beaming smiles.

Joey walked me up the aisle and I saw Danny's eyes fill with tears as he turned to watch our arrival. I may be a tiny bit biased, but it really was a beautiful service. Making our vows of lifelong commitment, hearing the prayers in Hebrew and English, standing beneath the flower-bedecked chuppa, it really felt like a joining of lives, of cultures, of fates. Afterwards as we, newly-wed, turned to walk back up the aisle together, the organ rang out the opening chords of *All You Need Is Love* and the entire congregation erupted into cheering applause. And I knew, absolutely without doubt, that this really was, just as it should be, the happiest day of my life.

At the reception Danny's speech revealed, for those who didn't already know, that I was carrying twins. He raised his glass and proposed a toast to 'Niki, and all the hearts that beat inside her'. I stood there beside my new husband and soulmate, surrounded by people who loved us and cruising on this huge wave of approval and, for the first time, I allowed myself to think that maybe it would really be OK after all.

The only sadness was that Simon pulled out on the wedding day morning. He had a last-minute panic attack, not entirely unexpectedly, and so Danny's close friend Bill stepped into the best-man breach in his place. It meant that we were left without anyone to represent the Shisler family but, as I said, it was clear that nothing could cloud our beautiful, joy-filled day. My wedding to Danny had been as perfect as a day can be; a real celebration of our love and our family. Going home after the party in a taxi with Joey in his suit and five-month-old Evie, asleep in my arms, in her teeny bridesmaid dress, we had everything to look forward to, a whole life together ahead of us. We were blessed.

~ 5 ~

With the wedding all done and dusted, I was free to get on with the serious business of growing two more babies. The first scan had revealed that both heartbeats were in the same little sac, meaning that my twins were from the same egg and therefore identical. The maternity hospital had a special twins clinic where I would be monitored with regular scans, and by seventeen weeks' gestation, I knew I was carrying boys. My online community was a wonderful source of advice and information, and I soon settled into the discussions and light-hearted banter that characterised the group. I still harboured serious concerns about my family's rapid expansion, but I was no longer raging with anger and fear.

Although this was my third pregnancy, and I should have been an old hand by now, a twin pregnancy is a very different experience from carrying a singleton. I'd already learned that a double dose of pregnancy hormones made for ferocious morning sickness, and that was far from the only surprise waiting to ambush me. I was soon vast: the gently rounded tummy that had been barely visible under my wedding dress rapidly morphed into a fully fledged baby bump and by four months I was already eliciting 'it won't be long now' comments from well-meaning strangers. Being almost full-term sized at not even halfway through the full nine months was actually quite frightening, and as someone who found much to complain about during a regular pregnancy, I was concerned that this was going to turn out to be a long, drawn-out and painful process for me and my poor beleaguered family as they vainly attempted to cheer, pacify and support me and my rapidly expanding bulk.

The Twins List was my lifeline. There, in the company of other twin parents and parents-to-be I could speak freely about the highs and lows of my situation. The other listees helped me plan for the birth and beyond, let off steam and vent frustration, deal with the myriad physical aches and niggles, and laugh at the ludicrousness, the sheer ridiculous comedy, of what was happening to my body. I *loved* being part of the group. As someone who often struggled in large social groups, who valued my privacy and enjoyed spending time alone, this was perfect. From the safety of my own home and at times of my own choosing, I could be the life and soul of this virtual party. It was fantastic: a social network that played to my strengths – an ability to express myself via the written word – and utterly ignored my weaknesses. Checking my email and writing to the list became an important feature of my day. I got to know the other mothers, learned their stories and followed their progress. The Twins List became my real-life soap opera, filled with drama, excitement, triumph and loss. There would be regular birth announcements as each pair of babies made its appearance, but there were sad times too. Infertility was an issue that many of the families on the list had struggled with and we would all ride the roller coaster with those going through treatments. Even when a pregnancy was confirmed, we knew that there were still dangers. One woman miscarried one of her twins and we all grieved with her as she came to terms with such a terrible loss. I was surprised by the intensity of my sorrow, for a woman I had never met. I can still vividly remember the cold, sickly shock as I read her dreadful news and the heartfelt tears that I cried for her and her baby. As I read the condolence emails from my listmates, each one echoing my own thoughts and feelings, I was grateful for the camaraderie and powerful sense of belonging. Even through such a terribly sad event, it was impossible not to feel uplifted by the strengths of the bonds between us all. Miscarriage was not the only worry for the pregnant mothers in the group, we knew that prematurity was a real risk with twins, and we sent love and prayers out to those mothers going through the nightmare of the NICU (neonatal intensive care unit). For some families, the undoubted pressure of having twins – physical, financial, emotional – proved too much and the group would see another sad divorce. Mainly though, it was a pretty cheerful slice of life. First steps and first teeth would be announced along with questions about potty training and debates about whether dressing twins alike was a good or bad thing.

At twenty weeks pregnant, just as I was finally reaching the point of acceptance about my situation, I was suddenly called in to the gynaecology clinic. A routine smear test had yielded some worrying results and the doctor needed to talk to me. Having had numerous friends go through the 'abnormal cells' situation, and having seen all of them resolved quickly and easily, I was not particularly concerned at my hospital summons. I walked the mile or so to the clinic, through the last of the autumn leaves, enjoying the crispness of the day and the wintry London sun. It occurred to me that I wouldn't be able to do this much longer; I would soon be too big to walk very far and then, I supposed, having three babies to care for was going to make such leisurely, solitary strolls a pretty rare commodity. I also realised that this thought no longer distressed me as it had only weeks ago. I can't say that it filled me with joy either, but there was a palpable softening of my attitude; I was definitely coming round to the idea of twins.

My mellow mood was abruptly shattered once I got in to see the doctor. She told me that my smear had, indeed, shown abnormal, pre-cancerous cell activity, but that the situation was somewhat graver than I, in my hormonal daze, had imagined. It seemed that the severity and scale of the changes had led her to conclude that my safest option was to be treated immediately, performing a cervical biopsy to remove the problematic cells, as well as all the surrounding tissue, before any cancer could get a firm hold. There was just one problem with this: it could not be done if I was pregnant.

It actually took a few moments for me to register what she was saying. I was being offered an abortion. At almost five months into my pregnancy, I was being strongly advised to terminate, in order to protect my own health. I couldn't take it in: the whole situation had suddenly become bizarrely surreal. I half-expected someone to laugh or reveal the hidden camera, it all seemed so unlikely, like a bad television drama.

I needed Danny; at that moment I needed him desperately. I was simply unable to know what the right thing to do was, or how to balance the needs of myself and my two existing children against the lives of the babies inside me. I called my husband who was, fortunately, working just minutes from the hospital and together we sat while the doctor again outlined the salient facts.

We were talking about degrees of risk. Left untreated until after the babies were born, it was most likely that my condition would remain localised and treatable. However, this could not be guaranteed. It was also possible that my pregnancy would accelerate the progression of the cancer to the point where, by the time the babies arrived, it would have reached my lymphatic system and it would be too late to be cured. Danny asked about statistics, how at risk was I *really*? She couldn't say: the risk was not big, but it was significant and real. We needed to make a decision, and quickly, about whether or not to proceed with the pregnancy.

It was Friday afternoon; the doctor agreed to give us the weekend to decide and we made an appointment for the following Monday morning. We were both incredibly shaken by this sudden turn of events that had thrown my entire pregnancy into a whole new light.

At home we talked, trying to work out the right thing to do. Danny told me that, ultimately, only I could really make the decision – it was, after all, my body, but I knew that he didn't want to lose the twins. And suddenly, for the first time, I realised that I didn't want to lose them either. For all my fear, all my doubts,

I wanted them. My children, my sons, they were precious to me, and there was no question about it: I could not harm them.

Later that night, as I sat in bed thinking about the day and listening to what my heart was telling me, I thought about the emotional distance I had travelled. From my first response of abject horror at the very idea of twins, I had finally reached a point where I wanted these babies as much as I had wanted Joey and Evie. It was ironic that it had taken the threat of losing them to show me that. The thing that I had thought I wanted, a chance to walk away from the pregnancy without shame or blame, had been given to me and, it turned out, it was not what I wanted at all. Yes, I knew that I could have gone ahead with an abortion and not a soul would have judged me harshly for it; I would have been completely justified in choosing not to risk my life. It was my door out, an emergency exit, at the last possible moment, and yet I couldn't bring myself to walk through it. I had made my choice freely. For better or worse, I'd joined this circus and committed my heart and I knew there was no turning back.

Courageous or foolhardy? I'm not sure it was either, really. My intuition told me that I would be OK, that the worrying cells inside me would still be containable at the end of my pregnancy. And, of course, the instinct to protect one's unborn child is very powerful.

Sometimes faith is the greatest gift of all, and I had that in abundance.

~ 6 ~

It was actually quite easy to put to one side any worries about my own health. Having made the decision to go ahead with the pregnancy, I saw no point in spending the next few months fretting about something over which I had no control. Part of the reason for my sanguine attitude was my lack of any time or energy for additional worrying.

We were having major building work done in our new house, involving new kitchen, bathrooms, old walls knocked down, new ones built, flooring changed and decoration throughout. It was hellish. I was desperate that it be finished before the boys were born; I hardly dared contemplate bringing two newborn babies home to a building site. Danny and I were completely new to this sort of operation, and we still had to learn that, in order to get an accurate idea of the work and money involved, you needed to take the builder's estimate with a shedload of salt by trebling the cost and quadrupling the time quoted. As each day ticked by, and I swelled to unimaginable size, I became steadily more anxious. Evie was still a long way from walking, and keeping her out of the builders' debris was becoming more and more challenging as I became less and less able to bend and lift. It was depressing and discouraging. The builders were useless and I was getting desperate. Despite the fact that I was heavily pregnant and also had a small baby to care for, we were left without even basic kitchen and bathroom facilities for weeks on end. As the time passed, I really started to panic.

To add to the pressure, Danny and I were well aware that, even with all work completed, the house would be far too small once the twins arrived. On discovering my new pregnancy, just weeks after moving in, we had agreed that, at a push, the new baby could share Evie's tiny bedroom for the first few years at least and then, eventually, we would sell up and get a bigger place. It would have been tight, but it was do-able. Twins, however, was an entirely different story. There was no way we could squish three kids into the minuscule space; the twins would have to room with us until, at the earliest possible opportunity, we could move somewhere bigger. Part of our remodelling had been the creation of a lovely walk-in wardrobe for me and Danny. Now, however, it had to be sacrificed as the only place left in the house which could contain a cot. The Twins List people assured me that the boys would be able to share a bed for the first six months at least, and I prayed they were right because there was really nowhere else for them to go.

The work was finally completed by the time I was seven months pregnant. I was absurdly big: the skin on my tummy was stretched so tightly over the little bundle of knees and elbows that it actually looked square, rather than the more usual rounded pregnancy shape. By now I was also in considerable discomfort for most of my waking hours. Walking was difficult; between the problems with balance and the ever-worsening sciatica, even crossing a room was tough. Breathing was restricted and uncomfortable; eating, near impossible. I was miserable beyond belief. And so was everyone around me.

We chose names for the babies: Theo William for the one the hospital was calling Twin A, Felix Samuel for the smaller Twin B. They wriggled around inside me much less than Evie or Joey had but then, I figured, they had a lot less room. I bought little outfits for them. I'd sworn I wouldn't dress them alike, but the potential cuteness factor was too big for me to ignore completely. In the end I compromised: they would have co-ordinated, rather than identical, clothes. I was actually surprised to be still pregnant at this stage. It seemed to be a fairly universal truth that twins came early and yet here I was, bigger than I had ever thought possible, with no sign of imminent delivery. My poor long-suffering family put up with week upon week of me groaning and creaking miserably, powerless to help. I watched my body like a hawk, desperate to find the first signs of labour. I was booked in for the elective Caesarean at thirty-eight weeks but I was hoping that my labour would kick off naturally somewhat earlier than that, forcing the hospital to operate before the appointed time.

I'd been having Braxton Hicks contractions (the 'painless' tightenings of the womb that mimic early labour without triggering birth) from around five months pregnant with the twins. With the double burden and stretching, I had found that many of the discomforts I experienced late in my previous pregnancies had pitched up a lot sooner, so the frequent bouts of Braxton Hicks were annoying but pretty well par for the course this time around. As Joey's birth had been induced and Evie's was pre-planned, I had never gone into labour naturally and this, combined with my overwhelming desire to have the pregnancy come to an end, had me wound up like a spring. My hospital bag had been packed for weeks, the house was finally finished, we'd engaged a childminder to help after the birth and the twins were mature enough to be born: I was ready. Poor Danny was just as desperate for it all to be over. Seeing me so miserable was hard enough; listening to my constant griping was undoubtedly painful and, naturally, he was also poised for action at a moment's notice, setting off for work each day with increasing trepidation.

At somewhere between thirty-five and thirty-six weeks I had my first brush with labour. The irregular Braxton Hicks contractions had, over the course of the day, settled into a regular five-minutes-apart pattern. They were painful too, enough so for me to have to catch my breath with each one. I called the hospital who told me to come straight down for monitoring. Once there, I was hooked up to the monitor that confirmed that, yes, I was having moderately strong contractions at five-minute intervals. The doctor's examination showed that I was only dilated a tiny bit; she decided that they would wait to see how things progressed before going ahead with the Caesarean. I was, after all, still less than thirty-six weeks pregnant; it would be better for the babies, I was told, if I could hang on to them a little longer. I was given gas and air to manage the pain and gradually, over the next few hours, the contractions weakened and then stopped. I was kept in hospital for observation overnight, spending it in huge discomfort attached to probes and monitors on an examination table in a side room of the labour ward. The following morning, feeling deflated emotionally, although, alas, not physically, I went home to continue my waiting.

False starts to labour are not uncommon so, although mightily frustrated, I was not especially surprised by this turn of events. My virtual friends sympathised and assured me that it really would all be over soon. I tried to keep focused on the babies that would soon be out of my belly and in my arms. I was feeling increasingly impatient though: each day of the pregnancy was a little harder than the day before. I felt like I had been pregnant forever.

Something *was* shifting within me though. A couple of days later I again found myself on my way to the hospital. This time I'd decided not to leave home until I was sure it was really labour and now, with contractions every four minutes, I was confident that this was it. I was nervous but also excited and relieved that the interminable waiting was almost over. At the hospital I was, again, monitored and examined. The contractions were fairly strong by this point and I was given a shot of pethidine for the pain. And again I watched in dismay as the powerful contractions gradually lessened and finally stopped altogether. After another depressing night spent wired up on the examination table, I was discharged again and slunk home embarassed, disappointed and exhausted, to wait for it to all start once more.

I didn't have to wait long. Later that day, with fingers crossed and praying that it would be third time lucky, I was headed back to the hospital's labour suite. I'd abandoned any semblance of dignity or reasonableness by this point and, as the contractions ebbed away, pleaded with the doctor on duty to send me to the operating theatre. I was treated with that politely patronising manner that doctors seem to reserve especially for pregnant women. How I refrained from punching him, I honestly don't know. The doctor explained slowly and patiently, as if to a difficult toddler, that it would be best for the babies if they could stay where they were for a bit longer. I was seething. Could they not see how desperate I was? I was in constant pain and the repeated labour scares had made me an emotional wreck. Nevertheless, he sent me home. He seemed completely unmoved by my begging.

This pattern continued for days. I would try to stay at home for as long as possible but, eventually, the contractions would get strong enough for me to go to the hospital. Once there, I would be monitored and examined but the contractions would gradually stop. I would sob and plead for them to deliver the babies to no avail, and would be sent home crushed, just in time for the whole thing to start up again. I was becoming increasingly desperate; I wanted the babies out and I felt sure that they wanted to be out. Day after day I would sit in the hospital, contorted by pain, crying with frustration, helpless, while doctors smiled at me and patted my hand and told me not to be impatient. A number of the midwives did take pity on me; they could see the terrible distress I was in and were sympathetic to my plight, but unfortunately the decision to deliver was not theirs to make, and I continued to rage hormonally at everyone.

Aside from the emotional pummelling this madness was giving me, it was also playing havoc with my family. Every visit to the hospital, with the possibility that *this* would be *it*, meant making arrangements for Joey and Evie's care, and dragging Danny out of his (thankfully understanding) office. My mother gamely pitched up every time, putting her own life on hold so she could take the reins of mine. We actually got quite skilled at setting the whole shebang in motion, but I think we ran out of excitement somewhere around the third time along. We even got to the point where my being admitted to hospital in labour was not, in itself, enough to make Danny leave work.

After a couple of weeks of this I was really freaking out. I *knew* the babies needed to be born although I didn't know how to articulate my sense of urgency in a way that would get the doctors to change their minds. They continued to treat me as though I was nothing more than impatient. Looking back now, on the last weeks of my pregnancy, it was all hazy and surreal. I knew and I didn't know that something was wrong. With hindsight it is clear to me that every scrap of maternal instinct was screaming that there was a problem but, at the time, I didn't know enough to trust myself and so allowed myself to believe what I was told: I was just a neurotic mother, overtired, overwrought and impatient.

I spent a lot of time in tears and even more strapped to one of those god-awful contraction monitors. It was always difficult to get a good trace of both babies' heartbeats: by the time one had been located and the probes had been attached to my tummy, the other one would have wriggled away so it was very rare for the doctors to get a clear look at how both babies were responding to this continuous stop-start labour.

Late one night I was, as usual, hanging out on the labour ward, praying that this time it wouldn't be a false alarm, that *this* time my boys would really be born. The duty doctor was one I hadn't seen before and at around ten o'clock he came in to look at the printout from the monitor. We had, by some fluke luck, managed to get a clear reading from both babies and the doctor was a bit concerned about Theo's readings. His heart-rate was a little irregular, an indication that he wasn't coping with the situation as well as we would have hoped. Perhaps this alone wouldn't have been enough to spur the doctor into action, but combined with my anxiety, my desperation and the fact that I had been effectively blocking a bed on the labour ward for around two weeks, it was enough to force his hand. The operating theatre was free, the anaesthetist was called and Danny was summoned to the hospital. He arrived within minutes and we were both gowned up. It was almost eleven o'clock; I felt shivery and anxious as I sat on the bed waiting to go down to theatre. Danny was excited and he hugged me reassuringly. But here I was, after weeks of begging doctors to deliver me, strangely unsettled.

I put my nerves down to tiredness more than anything; I *was* glad it was finally going to be over but I felt as though I was taking a step over the edge of a cliff. I turned to a beaming Danny and he kissed me. I smiled back and then we held hands as I was wheeled to the operating theatre. Showtime.

~ 7 ~

There are pivotal points in every life, moments or events that cause a seismic shift of such magnitude that they change not just everything that comes after them, but they even have the power to reach back into our past and change our perception of that which has gone before. Sometimes you can see these times coming: they are signposted, neon-lit and obvious. At other times it is only in retrospect that we can see that there was indeed a fork in the road, and our old life lies along the other path. Did I know as I stood at this great junction? Did I understand where I was, how much the world would change for me? Retrospection can be a distorting lens; it is not always easy to see the past clearly, as it really was. Emotion also blurs the edges of truth, I know this; and I have carried the emotional big guns: love, grief, fear, hope, despair; the grand cannons of the heart, making rubble of perception.

I remember everything. Each tiny moment as clear and brittle as glass, shards of crystal life suspended in a dream. Everything happened in slow motion, and a fingertip away from solid ground.

I am caught in waves, thickened and heavy, trapped in the treacle current, watching the tide unfold. Powerless.

My stomach lurches just with the memories; but I want to tell this story. I want to tell it like it was, to remind myself that it no longer is. Put the past in the past, close the door on it, finished.

* * *

The atmosphere in the operating theatre was quite different from when I'd had Evie, just twelve months earlier. Then there had been music playing and we had been buzzing with excitement. Now, though, I was exhausted and emotional. The past couple of weeks had been draining and the stress showed on both of us. The theatre was busy though, despite the late hour. Twins required a double team: two paediatricians, two midwives and, just in case, two little resuscitation trolleys. I wasn't worried though, at least I don't think I was; my twins were full term, and there was no reason to think that they wouldn't be ready.

Danny and I chatted as they administered the epidural and waited for it to take effect: some forced small talk, as he tried to keep my mind off the comedy-gruesome needle they use to puncture your spine. I probably made some smart-arse comments; bitch-humour is often my fallback position in times of anxiety (and having one's body sliced open by a stranger, however well-meaning, is surely high on anyone's list of anxious moments). From behind the screen, the doctor was critical of my previous Caesarean scar and promised a prettier finish this time round. I remember saying that maybe they should just put a zip in: I'd been opened up so many times. And then, suddenly, Theo was out!

There was a flurry of activity: Theo was not breathing well and seemed unresponsive. He was taken to the resuscitation table and Danny left my side to go with him. From my prone position it was hard to make out much of what was going on, but then Danny was at my side, holding Theo, showing me our son. I barely got a glimpse of him before the midwife came to take him back, but there was no time to fret because Felix appeared. In the excitement, I hadn't even noticed them taking him out of me, but now here he was, squawking and angry and absolutely tiny in his daddy's arms.

Felix seemed fine but the paediatrician announced that Theo needed to go to special care. Somewhere along the line, my mother and brother had arrived at the hospital and Danny dispatched them to accompany Theo to the NICU (neonatal intensive care unit) while he stayed with Felix and me.

By the time I was stitched up and settled in my room, it was the early hours of the morning. Charlie and my mother had joined us and brought reassuring news of Theo. The NICU team had told them that he just needed a bit of help but would, no doubt, be fine within a few days. The babies were good weights for twins: Felix was just over five pounds and Theo, I was amazed to hear, was a massive six pounds and fourteen ounces! As it turned out, several weeks later, Theo had actually gained a pound in the translation of metric to imperial measures, but he was still the bigger of the two and, at just a shade under six pounds, a pretty decent size for a twin. I had delivered eleven pounds of baby, along with two lots of amniotic fluid and two placentas: no wonder I had complained.

In bed, after everyone had gone, and basking in the warm glow of the morphine I'd been given, I got my first chance to have a proper look at Felix. He was the scrawniest little scrap I'd ever seen: he had so little body fat that even his skin seemed too big, sitting in baggy little folds around his tiny knees and elbows. I smiled at his comical face – 'Bless his heart,' I thought. 'He'll need to grow into that nose.' And he did indeed have the funniest Jewish comedy-nose you could imagine. I was right too; it was just his skinniness that made his nose look so big. These days he has a lovely (and tiny) button nose that fits his face perfectly.

He began to cry, a funny little mewling noise, and I got him latched on to feed. He was lovely and though my heart easily stretched to encompass him, I didn't feel that same sense of joyful elation that I'd had after Joey's or Evie's births. I put my feelings of disquiet down to the trauma of the past few weeks, the lateness of the hour and, of course, the fact that Theo was in the NICU on the other side of the hospital. I couldn't think about Theo: I had a baby at my breast, and I couldn't register the existence of another child. It was too hard to comprehend. Right at that moment, my whole world comprised just Felix and me; post-delivery bonding was in full throttle and I couldn't have resisted it if I tried. There was guilt too: my conscious brain knew that Theo was missing, and rationalised that I should have been more disturbed by the separation than I was, but the combination of hormones, drugs and exhaustion was more than enough to silence the voice of doubt.

After suckling for a few minutes, Felix fell asleep. I tried all the usual tricks to wake a feeding baby but he was out cold. He'd fallen asleep at the breast on every feed so far and I guessed that his tiny size meant we'd be doing lots of very short feeds, at least until he grew bit.

Danny had been to see Theo and had brought me a blurry Polaroid of him to keep by my bed. He was covered with probes and wires, his face completely obscured by the ventilator tubing: it could, quite frankly, have been anyone, but I loyally propped it up on my bedside table and tried not to worry about the fact that I was bonding with only one of my babies.

The following morning brought the rest of the family visitors and over the course of the day a stream of people bounced between me and Felix on the top floor of the hospital, and Theo who was still downstairs in the NICU. I was not allowed to go down there myself, being so recently post-operative. I had only been able to manage a few faltering steps to the bathroom, so a trip to the other side of the hospital was out of the question. Theo was doing fine, according to reports, and would soon be off the ventilator and I was expressing milk for him to be given as soon as he was strong enough. In truth, although it feels shameful to even acknowledge this now, I was actually feeling quite resentful towards Theo. I can remember cuddling Felix and wishing that Theo didn't exist: without him life became much more straight-forward and uncomplicated. Having Theo meant acknowledging fear, doubt and danger.

In mitigation for my apparent callousness, I will say that the days following the birth of a child are not a time of clear thinking for a mother. It is a primitive, animalistic state which, for all the undoubted joy, is also traumatic both physically and emotionally. Having the child that you have grown and protected inside you suddenly outside of your body and exposed to the world feels as vulnerable as if it was one of your internal organs that was on show. The connection between mother and baby remains very powerful in the days following delivery. For me, the need to see and touch my newborn is always as intense and as physical as hunger. In this case, however, even though I had barely seen Theo, Felix was right here, at the centre of my awareness and satisfying my baby-lust all by himself. My instincts and maternal urges were following their usual pattern as I connected with Felix alone. I had no idea how to handle having an absent baby, though, and at that particular moment, it was hard not to see the superfluous Theo as just a bewildering irritant.

Danny had been despatched on the first night to announce the boys' birth to my friends on the Twins List. He'd arrived at hospital the following morning with a sheaf of congratulatory emails and reassurances from around the world that we would all be together soon enough. I knew that I was not unusual, that twins often needed that little bit of extra help, but reading the letters, full of tales of early-day hiccoughs and bumpy starts, helped to soothe me and partially quieten the insistent sound of an alarm bell ringing somewhere deep in my psyche.

At around thirty-six hours post-operatively, I was finally deemed well enough to make my first visit to see Theo in the NICU. I held Felix and Danny pushed my wheelchair to the lift that would take us down to him. In a maternity hospital, as you might imagine, a pyjama-clad mother clutching a tiny ball of newborn is a common sight and we received the indulgent smiles of our fellow travellers in the lift. Everyone held something:

flowers, a teddy bear, the ubiquitous BabyGap bag; but I was the only one with an actual baby in my arms. Despite the approving looks and little 'ahh bless' coos of congratulation, despite the fact that I had no relationship with these people beyond these few moments we were spending together between floors, I felt short-changed. I wanted them to know that Felix, my cute little button boy, was only half the story. Suddenly having *a* baby seemed ordinary and prosaic: I wanted acknowledgement of my achievement and recognition for my new status, as a mother of twins.

The NICU is a different world, closed off from the rest of the hospital and operating under different rules. We waited at the door under the watchful eye of the security camera, for clearance to enter the unit. We were buzzed in and a nurse met us at the door. There were a number of nurseries, little rooms holding between three and six cots, all leading off a long corridor. The intensive care units, with incubators for the frailest babies, were at the far end, followed by the high dependency room, then 'special care' and finally nurseries for those who would soon be going home. The rooms mirrored their little patients' progress, each downgrade in level of support being literally and symbolically a step nearer to the door. Theo was in the very furthest room: we had a long way to go.

The regular bulletins I'd been getting while on the ward had been full of reassurance: he just needed a bit of help and would be joining Felix and me very soon. Now, however, I was being told by an earnest young doctor to 'prepare myself and to try not to be upset'. I was taken to Theo's cot. My little baby boy's face was completely obscured by the tape that was holding the ventilator tube in place, and the blindfold that was to protect his eyes from the harsh lights. He was naked, lying on his back, under warming lights. I was shocked to see that his little chest was rising and falling rapidly, as though he was panting or hyperventilating: he had been put on the vile oscillating ventilator that I had heard some of the twin mothers, those who had delivered very early, mention. I was confused – my babies weren't micro-preemies (the term often used to describe extremely premature babies); actually they were technically not really preemies at all. Surely this ventilator was used for those whose lungs had not yet matured? The doctor agreed that it was unusual for a baby of Theo's gestational age to have immature lungs but, he told me, twins are often a bit different, throwing up anomalous results, and maybe we'd got my dates wrong anyway. Essentially though, I was assured, it looked worse than it really was and Theo was sedated and therefore not in any discomfort, despite appearances. In any case, they were quite certain he would be off the vent soon.

I looked at my baby and my heart ached for him. He looked pitiful; much littler than I'd expected (of course, at this point I still thought he was a whole pound heavier than he turned out to be) with a bewildering array of tubes and wires emanating from his tiny frame. Lights and numbers beeped and flashed on the front of huge pieces of equipment many, many times the size of my son. A nurse wearing surgical scrubs moved silently around the cot adjusting dials and jotting down notes; the air hummed with the sound of machinery.

Motherhood hit me like brick: the missing emotion and attachment to Theo sprang, fully-formed, into my consciousness.

Now I was here, now *he* was here, all the pain of our separation engulfed me with its realness and the tears came hard and fast. I lay my head on the mattress, bringing my face as close as possible to Theo's little blindfolded one and I stroked his minute hand. He, of course, was far too sedated to respond and it was clear that, whilst the nurses were never anything but welcoming and supportive, I was really somewhat in the way; but, at that moment, I needed the touch far more than he did, and the NICU staff had seen enough post-natal mothers to know this.

It was hard to be back in my room afterwards. Prior to the NICU visit, I had coped with Theo's absence by essentially pretending he didn't exist; it was all about me and Felix. Now, though, I was torn between them and seeing Theo had brought all my anxieties to the surface. In fact, now I was actually more worried about him and, in addition to my fears, I was carrying a lot of guilt. Was it my fault? Had I pushed the hospital to deliver the babies before they were really ready? Why couldn't I have just been patient, why did I have to be so bloody selfish? These thoughts ran repeatedly through my mind, torturing me into a self-flagellating emotional frenzy, which was aided and abetted by the arrival of my double dose of post-partum hormones, the baby blues.

I tried to keep myself occupied with Felix who was actually turning out to be quite a high-maintenance child himself. He seemed to be unable to stay awake through a feed. I would put him on the breast but after a few minutes he would fall asleep, only to wake up screaming with hunger the minute I put him down. Despite his scrawniness and his tiny voice, he was more than capable of making his feelings known. Danny and I would laugh at his comical rage: he was so little, so quiet and yet he would get so very *cross*, as if he had the emotions of a vastly bigger baby. I have photographs from the hospital of Felix in all his baggy-kneed, raging fury; now, when I look at them, I want to cry with shame at my earlier ignorance. Felix was screaming his desperation at us, his parents, and we just thought it was funny.

The NICU had sent me up an electric breast pump, a bizarre and intimidating suction-contraption that looked like it had come straight from a dairy farm, and seemed to have been designed to collect milk in the most painful and humiliating way possible. This, along with the fact that Felix needed to be fed almost continuously, meant that I was rarely without something attached to my breast and my definition of acceptably polite behaviour had to be rapidly expanded to incorporate public (partial) nudity. It was not that long since I'd been breastfeeding Evie, so it took almost no time for me to re-establish a good supply of milk. I'm one of those women who enjoys breastfeeding and, by this stage in my parenting life, I was good at it. Whilst most of the other mothers on the NICU were struggling to produce a few thimblefuls of breast milk, I would pitch up smugly to hand in my couple of full bottles per day.

Some memories are more difficult than others. Again, for me, it is hindsight that makes certain incidents hard to bear. When Felix was a couple of days old I had a run in with one of the hospital's paediatricians. Whilst running standard checks on him, she had found his blood sugar to be low, implying that he was not getting enough to eat. I, already post-natal, tearful and stressed, was enraged. How *dare* this doctor, little more than a child herself, suggest that I wasn't feeding my baby properly or enough! Felix was fine! Theo was the sick one; I'd had four children, I knew what I was talking about. Could she take him to be weighed? No! I wasn't letting her touch him: she clearly knew nothing. I was astounded that this ignorant woman was actually a paediatrician! I am not, by nature, prone to temper, or even anger: even my immediate family have only very rarely seen me let rip. This outburst was so out of character that even the copious amounts of drugs and hormones swilling around my system couldn't quite explain my behaviour. Danny comforted me as I sat trembling on the bed, ranting about ill-trained, insensitive medical staff whilst desperately trying to get my poor beleaguered Felix to wake up enough to actually feed.

Denial: yes, I know, it's obvious *now*. But in that hormone-hazy, surreal space nothing made much sense. I had started this pregnancy emotionally adrift but, through seemingly Herculean effort, I had eventually hauled myself on to an even keel. It had taken time and patience but I had regained my peace of mind, found acceptance and had even come to be excited and delighted that I was having twins. Over the last few weeks of the pregnancy I could feel that hard-won equanimity slipping away and now, with Theo in intensive care and my growing sense that something was not right, it felt as though an ever-deepening fog had descended; nothing was clear, reality felt muffled and hard to discern. I was exhausted, both physically and emotionally, sore-eyed from crying and heavy with milk. I desperately needed to believe that Felix was fine. I absolutely could not countenance any more uncertainty.

It was suggested we tried cup-feeding Felix, just in case he wasn't getting enough milk from the breast. I didn't want to give him a bottle and so this was the next best solution. Danny sat as instructed trying to keep the tiny, and seemingly boneless, Felix upright on his lap. Gingerly he managed to pour a little of my expressed milk into his son's mouth. Felix fell asleep almost immediately: this clearly wasn't going to work.

Whilst we struggled to get more calories into Felix up on the ward, Theo was making good progress in the NICU. He'd come off the oscillating ventilator and had been downgraded to a CPAP – a much less invasive and gentler form of respiratory support. The CPAP involved a corrugated tube that came over his head and blew air up his nose. The tubing was held in place by being tied to a little woolly hat. The hospital has hundreds of these hats, in various shades of pink, blue and lemon, obviously knitted by a small army of local grandmothers and donated to the NICU 'for the little ones'. Theo looked incredibly silly in his pink bonnet (despite the careful colour-coding devised by the grandma army, the hospital seemed utterly incapable of putting anything but pink hats on Theo), but also very sweet, and it was great to see that he was making progress. Everyone seemed happy with how he was doing and, though I knew we would not all be able to leave hospital together, everyone assured me that Theo would not be too far behind us. It was hard not being able to cuddle him and I was still feeling a lot of guilt about bonding with Felix without Theo but, as the days passed and my hormone levels started to get back to normal, it was all getting a little easier to bear, with longer intervals between the inevitable teary spells.

Felix and I went home four days after the birth. I was sore but desperate to get out of the hospital; I knew I'd heal much quicker at home where I could relax and look after myself. It was tough leaving Theo but, as his discharge could still be a couple of weeks away, there was no other option. I marshalled my family into a crack Theo-visiting squad: my baby might have to stay in the hospital, but he didn't have to be alone. I knew that having people there who loved him and could stroke his little hands and sing him lullabies would speed his recovery. My mum, Charlie, Pierre, and even Danny's mother when she could, would take it in turns to sit by his incubator and will him better.

At home the reality of the situation hit me for the first time. Evie was staying with my mother while I recovered from my surgery, Felix was there with me and Theo was still in the hospital. That night I wrote to the Twins List:

> 'My three littlest babies, in three different places and all needing so much in so many different ways. Where do you leave your heart? Sometimes I feel overwhelmed and so unequal to this task but today I managed to spend some time with each of them and for a little bit it felt more manageable. I know that we will all be together soon and pray that it won't be too long.'

Once again, just the act of unburdening myself in writing had a hugely calming effect. Some of my online friends, mainly the Europeans, responded immediately and emails of support continued to drop into my inbox throughout the night as first the

Eastern seaboard, then the central states and, finally, the West Coast of America woke up to my *cri de coeur*.

I felt awful for Theo; it seemed to me that his life was getting off to the worst possible start. As a newborn, he should have been in his mother's arms, surrounded by love, comfort and security. Instead he was alone in the harshly clinical environment of the NICU. His first experiences had been of pain, fear and aloneness and I beat myself mercilessly for this. Theo's failure to manage without respiratory help was something of a mystery to the doctors, but I felt certain it was something I had done or failed to do. Maybe it was a manifestation of my initial hostility to the pregnancy, or was it my childish, desperate lack of patience in the last weeks before the birth. I didn't know how, but I did know, beyond a shadow of a doubt, that it was a direct result of my parental failings.

Theo got sick. On top of everything else he succumbed to one of the many bugs that lurk in hospitals, using the steady supply of vulnerable and compromised humans to spread and strengthen. Having slowly got Theo to the point of tolerating small amounts of my breast milk in his tummy, we were suddenly back to square one, with him allowed nothing but water and antibiotics. It was incredibly frustrating; especially trying to break the cycle of weakness and feeding problems. We *were* moving forward, the doctors assured me, albeit agonisingly slowly. Again and again I was counselled to be patient and to remember that, in the grand scheme of a lifetime with my children, this little sojourn was utterly insignificant.

Felix, meanwhile, was proving to have some idiosyncrasies of his own. Everything about him was tiny: his size, his appetite, his cry. He was like a scaled-down version of a baby. His funny, weedy little cry soon earned him his first nickname: Squeak-a-Mouse. Danny even found the theme tune to Danger Mouse online, and downloaded it (*He's astounding, he's amazing, whenever there is danger he'll be there!*) so we could sing it to a completely bemused Felix at bath time. Feeding him, though, was turning out to be an epic task with him needing milk almost hourly, and around the clock. He also seemed to have a powerful aversion to being put down. Felix was only settled when he was being held, something I, at that point, put down to his being a twin. Identical twins come from the same egg, springing into existence at the exact same moment. There is for them not even one millisecond of solitude and maybe, I reasoned, this was why Felix had such a powerful need for physical human contact. In fact, as it turned out, this terror of being left, even for a second, was actually an early manifestation of our son's incredible survival instinct.

I ventured out with him a couple of times but his tinyness frightened me and I felt too exposed and vulnerable with such a wee thing out in public. In addition to his minuscule size, Felix was also still very floppy. The baby carrier was hopeless; I would strap him to me, as I had with Joey and Evie, only to see him immediately melt into a little puddle of baby inside the harness. Unlike Evie, who had managed to hold her head up from practically her first day, Felix appeared to have a spine made of Play-Doh.

On top of my anxiety about Theo and the fact that Felix was also turning out to be a rather complicated baby, I had Evie to worry about. Since the boys had been born she'd been staying with my mother, but now, with Felix a week old, I was desperate to get her home. Evie, of course, was still very much a baby herself: just a year old, not yet walking and able to say only a couple of words, it was almost impossible for her to understand what was going on. She'd spent a little time with Felix and me and, despite her lack of language skills, had managed to make her feelings about this new, mummy-stealing interloper perfectly clear. In the end her hostility to her new brother did soften somewhat, especially when she was allowed to spend seemingly endless hours pulling off his little socks as fast as I could replace them. My cunning plan was to get her used to Felix and then, when Theo came home, she might not notice that her brother had suddenly doubled.

I can remember, with absolute clarity, the first time I saw Theo's face properly. For the first week of his life his face was partially obscured by ventilator tubing and adhesive tape until, one day, I went in for my regular visit and there he was, tubeless, bonnet-less and awake in his little cot. The nurses disentangled the mass of wires and probes that were attached to him and placed him gently into my arms. I bent my head to kiss his little face, bursting with joy and love as this much-delayed meeting finally took place, and then I saw it. I saw the disability, saw that he was not OK. He was just as beautiful but I can remember clearly thinking that he looked like a disabled child. I didn't know the term 'myopathic features' at this stage, and in any case I'm not sure that I would have even been able to articulate what was wrong, just that something about this beautiful child had set my maternal alarm ringing.

But I still didn't know. A hundred little hints, a thousand times I saw without seeing, heard without hearing, knew and didn't know. I can't explain, truly I don't think that it was fear or shame that stopped me short of realisation every single time. No, I think it was more the utter unlikeliness of the truth because I was, of course, at this point still living in a world where things like this didn't happen to people like me. So I brushed awareness from my mind, little crumbs of knowledge swept away without a thought.

Theo continued to improve as a full feeding regime was finally instated. He was still being fed mostly by naso-gastric tube with the nurses giving him an occasional bottle of my breast milk. Eventually, with Theo breathing without help at last, I was told I would be allowed to give him his first breast feed. I was overjoyed. This, at last, felt like real progress; concrete evidence that my baby was getting better, and I could barely contain my excitement.

If only it were that simple. Everyone agreed that Theo was ready to feed naturally, but no one seemed to have alerted him to this fact and, after ten days of being fed entirely by tube, he had not the first clue about what to do. I held him to me and wept tears of utter frustration as his surprised little face looked up at me quizzically, my nipple sitting uselessly in his mouth. How could I show him what to do, that he needed to suck if he was to get food? Just as I was about to give up, Felix, sitting in his car seat at my feet, let out his weedy-cat-cry and my body responded as the body of a lactating woman always does to the squawk of her infant, by letting go a trickle of milk into Theo's waiting mouth. He got the hint and began to feed: we were off! We must have made quite a sight that day, me tear-stained and laughing, scrap-like Felix squeaking at my feet and a very surprised-looking Theo at my breast. My boys were a teeny tag team, achieving together something that they could not manage alone.

My family were fantastic and took their Theo-visiting duties very seriously. I think there was barely a minute of the day or night that he didn't have someone sitting by his cot, trying to beam positive thoughts at him. Knowing that he was getting so much love from his extended family made me feel slightly less guilty about having bonded so much better with Felix. With all my family getting so involved in his progress, he was clearly going to hold a special place in all their hearts. It was some small compensation although, of course, I did continue to worry that Theo would suffer some long-term trauma due to early maternal separation and sibling envy.

Felix continued to be adorable, and so tiny he barely seemed real. It amazed me that something so small could be an actual person, and the skin on his minute cheeks was so soft that you could barely feel it when you kissed him. I still felt incredibly nervous and clumsy around him which surprised me because, even though he was very small, I was pretty experienced with babies and had expected to be quite laid-back about my third and fourth children.

Thirteen days after the twins' birth all my anxiety about Felix finally focused into a tangible concern. I fed him as usual in the morning but he was clearly not well. He was grey-skinned and even floppier than usual with laboured and raspy breathing. Danny and I threw on clothes and headed for the hospital. By the time we arrived at the NICU Felix was clearly very sick. I handed him over to Theo's paediatrician who took one look at him before making the decision to admit him immediately. Under normal circumstances, we were told, a baby who had been home would not be admitted to the NICU and Felix should have been sent to the PICU (Paediatric Intensive Care Unit) which was actually in another hospital. But, in view of the fact that Theo was already in residence, and out of compassion for Danny and me, they agreed to waive the rules for Felix.

I was grateful for this small mercy. Reeling with shock and nauseous with fear for my poorly little one, I could not have begun to contemplate having the boys in different hospitals. Danny took me home to the house where there was now just one of my children, rather than the four I had been expecting to have around me by this stage. I wrote to the Twins List:

> 'They say it's two steps forward and one step back but today it doesn't seem that way. Theo has been making slow but steady progress, still in intensive care but gaining weight and spending longer periods breathing unaided. I had planned to bring my one-year-old, Evie, home tomorrow so that, despite Theo being in hospital, we could start to return to something like a normal family life.
>
> This morning Felix took ill. Choking when I fed him and stopping breathing. I knew that something was wrong so I took him into hospital and they have admitted him to intensive care. They're not quite sure what's wrong with him yet but he's in an incubator, hooked up to drips, antibiotics, CPAP machine for his breathing – just where Theo was this time last week. I am devastated – I didn't

*realise how much having Felix at home with me was help-ing to make Theo's absence bearable. Walking out of the hospital with his empty car seat, leaving my little ones behind, was the hardest thing I have ever done in my life. I am trying so hard to stay calm and strong for my family but I feel like every cell in my body is screaming for my babies. Now I can't even hold Felix and he **hates** to be alone. I am praying hard for the strength to cope with this but it is slow to come. I had got used to having Theo in the hospital; it was still upsetting but somehow manageable. Felix going in is such a shock and it seems as though our whole world has turned upside down again.*

I don't know how to do this. I am pumping every two hours for them, spending as much time as possible with them, singing to them, talking, stroking them and it just doesn't seem enough.'

And then I lay on my bed and cried myself to sleep.

~ 8 ~

Another world. Most of the time we live our lives within carefully constructed and clearly defined parameters – what we know, where we go, even who we are – all bound by our range of experience and knowledge, and by the choices we make. Then one day, we open a door and find ourselves somewhere completely new, somewhere that we barely even knew existed. In this newly discovered parallel universe, we are all adrift. Instead of the familiarity of home and the autopilot existence of our regular lives, we have a new terrain to learn, new paths to build, new rules to understand and people to meet. When I opened the door to the NICU, I stepped into another world. Already disoriented by being separated from my babies, I now had to find a route through this new-found land.

There are few places where you can witness more raw emotion than a NICU. The air is thick with hormonal fog; day and night melt into each other. It is the twilight zone, with added babies. The sense of disconnection from the real world is profound and starts the moment you walk through the door. Nothing is left to chance in a NICU: the tiny lives of its tenants are too fragile for uncertainty, so the door is kept locked and each desperate visitor is scanned and sorted via the emotionless eye of the CCTV before the door is opened.

Life sits on a knife-edge here, stretching the limits of what is possible, making ordinary that which is miraculous, defining and redefining what constitutes hope, success and even life. There are the tiniest ones: little splinters of scrawn and fluff. Twenty-five weeks along or twenty-four ... or twenty-three. You've seen the pictures, scraps of barely-humanness beset by tubes and tapes, just a pound – *nothing*, a feather; watched over by shell-shocked parents who are too frightened even to cry properly. They sit while silent tears etch the lines on their faces that will remain years from now, invisible but ever-present; marked for life by this time. They tell you it's a roller-coaster and you think you understand that this means up and down; it turns out to mean so much more. There is the breath-holding, fingers-crossed, inch-by-bloody-inch progress before the acrid nausea of a fall. And, of course, you can't get off: once you board the ride, you're there until the end, but no one can tell you when that will be. Maybe it's best that way.

The doctor diagnosed Felix as having a virus that had blossomed into pneumonia. His chest sounded terrible through the stethoscope and he was struggling to breathe. It was heartbreaking seeing him hooked up to the machines and monitors and I was devastated. I'd got used to seeing Theo like that, and had rationalised that, as he'd never known anything else, it wouldn't be too traumatic for him. Felix though, was a different story. Felix had been at home, surrounded by love and attention; would he think that we had abandoned him? And even though I knew that he was far too young to really register or understand his change of surroundings, I fretted nonetheless about future attachment and commitment problems brought on by this bumpy start. My child was less than three weeks old and I was already foreseeing a life of heart-break and loneliness (and probably alcoholism at the very least, as he tried to drown out the scream of his inevitably low self-esteem). I wisely kept my fears for my sons' emotionally crippled futures to myself, figuring that I would be judged as being just a touch neurotic if I shared these thoughts with any medical staff.

With both boys in incubators and using ventilators (Felix full-time, Theo part-time) in the very furthest room from the door, we were as far from going home as we'd ever been and it was getting harder and harder to see how that might change. The boys' continuing failure to thrive was as mysterious as ever. Every day the doctors would come up with another list of possible illnesses, syndromes and conditions and another battery of tests would be run on blood or body parts only to come back negative. Felix and Theo's little heels were raw and swollen from the endless needle sticks to collect blood samples, and I was grateful that at least there were two of them to share the painful jabs and torments, but still we had no answers. 'No news is good news,' the doctors would say. 'We might never know what it was. They'll probably grow out of it/get better and you'll never be any the wiser.' But I knew that they were really as frustrated as I was, and perplexed by their own inability to get my babies well.

I became part of the NICU world, forming unspoken bonds with the other parents in my part of the unit. There was always someone in a worse position than you. I remember seeing a family's devastation as they were told their daughter's cleft palate was just the most obvious symptom of a deeper and darker syndrome. The palate could be fixed, but their child's other problems were profound and lifelong. I saw them struggle to comprehend the implications as they slowly absorbed the fact that their daughter was disabled. My heart ached for the poor parents and I silently thanked God that, eventually, we would be able to put this entire episode behind us and get on with our lives as a family.

I fell into a routine. I would spend the morning with Evie before handing her over to my childminder and making the fifteen-minute walk to the hospital. I've always loved to walk in London and now spring was breaking even here, in the heart of the urban jungle. I have one of the most complex internal jukeboxes (that strange mechanism that plays songs in your head) of anyone I know: the soundtrack to my life is virtually constant, hugely eclectic and I have a near-perfect recall of just about every song I've ever heard (this is more of a curse than a blessing). Walking, the rhythm of my footsteps on the pavement, is prime internal-singing time for me and the music that accompanied me for most of those trips to the hospital was TLC's *No Scrubs* which was a huge hit at the time. It fitted because, even though the song tells us that '*a scrub is a man who can't get no love from me*', in my mind it became about the clinical blue and green uniforms worn by the NICU staff. '*I don't want no scrubs*,' I would chant to myself and smile at the weird appropriateness of the current number one.

Theo was the first to graduate from intensive care, making the hugely symbolic leap into the special care nursery one night while I was at home. I arrived at the hospital the following morning to find my sweet boy one room closer to the door and lying in an ordinary hospital cot. Although he still had his feeding tube in place the nurses told me he had not yet been given his milk: would I like to breastfeed him? They didn't have to ask twice; I had Theo out of his cot and latched on in the blink of an eye, certainly before any doctor passed by and nixed the idea (as they were prone to do). Theo fed for around ten minutes and I was in heaven. The simple acts of normal mothering had become such a luxury for me that I needed to savour every second. My tiny Theo didn't seem particularly awed by the occasion but, nonetheless, I whispered stories of home and spontaneity into his little ear; I wanted to tell him about the world outside the NICU, the only thing he had ever known, as if this would motivate a weeks-old baby to get well.

When Felix also graduated from intensive care the very next day, I was ecstatic. Now it really felt like we were making progress. I virtually danced my way to the hospital and I suspect that my accompanying 'internal singing' may have actually externalised, which must have made me a bizarre sight as I sang and danced my way through the busy streets. I guess I was already learning to grab my joy where I could but I certainly did have every reason to be hopeful.

With both babies out of incubators and breathing alone (although still requiring oxygen) handling them became a million times easier. Up until this point, even getting a cuddle with one of the babies was a major operation. I would have to sit stock-still on a hard chair, while the nurses arranged baby, blankets, tubes and wires around me. By the time everything had been properly moved and disconnected/reconnected, I would be starting to cramp and the baby would be asleep. It was such a production that I rarely even asked to get them out. Now, though, I could pick them up easily whenever I wanted. Such luxury: I could be spontaneous! My nightly missive to the Twins List made clear my delight.

> '*My babies are getting better, London is blessed with beautiful spring sunshine and I'm not pregnant any more. Life is looking up...*'

And there was more delight; now that the babies were off the critical list it wasn't just me getting cuddles. They also had each other and the doctors agreed to let them spend their days snuggled together in the same cot. I knew that this would help them get better: after all, physical proximity was the norm for twins, and it was being alone that was strange. I also hoped that this contact would, in some way, be compensation for not having me there. They could be each other's substitute mummy.

Individually Felix and Theo were lovely babies, full of character, charm and joy despite their undoubtedly grim welcome to the world, but put together there was an exponential leap in their loveliness. My little Gestalt boys – so much greater than the sum of their parts. Watching them cuddle and play together, my heart seemed to flip right over with joy and pride. I was utterly enchanted by them and quite overwhelmed by their cuteness. And, for the first time, I could really see how alike they were. Of course, identical twins, what did I expect? Even so, it still seemed extraordinary and magical to me and it was hard to believe that I had actually played a part in this miracle myself. The boys *loved* being together too: they hugged and snuggled against each other and even, most adorably of all, sucked each other's thumbs. I was awash with love for them and that love, along with a double dose of maternal pride, helped carry me through the frustration of those early weeks.

*'Well we're still on the special care roller coaster. Both boys are still in hospital but they **are** making progress (albeit, painfully slow...)'*

The journey itself was nothing if not unpredictable. We would have a good day, with some weight gain and long periods of unaided breathing, and I would be euphoric. Then we'd have a bad day and it would all seem so much harder. Most of the time I managed to hold up OK, but at other times I would feel completely emotionally exhausted. It felt as though I had been somehow dropped into the wrong life. I had expected, by this point, to be sleep-deprived, up to my ears in nappies, surrounded by dirty dishes and dirty laundry in huge, equally neglected piles. Instead, I found myself child-free, walking through the streets around my home. I wanted a badge to wear, that said 'I just had *twins*, I have *four* kids'. I knew it didn't make much sense, but there were times when I even felt angry that everything I was going through, momentous as it was to me, was actually invisible to the rest of the world. Only my friends in cyberspace saw the real life I was living, the juggling of priorities and the struggle to maintain an even keel, for the sake of *all* of my children.

> '*Even this situation has become routine. Visiting hospital, three-hourly pumping, fitting in the shopping and the cooking, playing with Evie, checking Joey did his home-work. I try to keep everything normal and then it strikes me that this **isn't** normal and...*'

My babies were beautiful, though; they had Danny's long, delicate fingers and the most gorgeous, almond-shaped, blue-grey (eventually to be brown) eyes, and they really did seem to be getting better. They were both in cots, rather than incubators, by this point and I was even able to breastfeed them occasionally. While Joey and Evie look a lot like me (and in Evie's case the resemblance is quite uncanny), Felix and Theo were taking after their father's side of the family. Theo, the slightly bigger and heavier of the two, looked especially like Danny's brother, Simon, whereas Felix looked like Danny. It was funny, I had never been able to see the family resemblance between Danny and Simon before, but now, looking at the twins, it was easy to see the common features between them all.

I got to know some of the other mothers a little, at least those whose babies were sharing a nursery with mine. They are odd little friendships you have in the NICU, based so much more on the unspoken understanding between women, than on any actual knowledge of each other. There was, perhaps, little to say and we rarely talked about our life outside, but the wan smiles of greeting, the not needing to explain each unexpected bout of tears and the shared celebration at the tiniest whisper of progress made for some powerful bonding. A mother's separation from her newborn is so physically and emotionally unnatural; we didn't need words to share our thoughts.

Whilst the doctors' official line on the boys remained that they were just a bit 'small and weedy' and would probably grow out of it and be fine, Danny and I were starting to hear the first signs of some deeper medical concerns. I lost count of the number of times we were asked if we were related ('are you *sure*?') which would increase the probability of a genetic aberration. For us it was, of course, a question loaded with irony. No, we explained, the chances of Danny and me being related were vanishingly small. My non-Jewishness was a pretty cast-iron indicator that we were not from the same gene pool and we could definitely strike inbreeding from the list of things that might have gone wrong.

We were starting to get our first labels around this time too. 'Hypotonia' or low muscle tone was the first one; and then 'bulbar palsy' meaning a weakness specifically of the bulbar region (face, mouth, throat). 'Aspiration' was another word that cropped up frequently, meaning that milk supposedly destined for the stomach was actually getting into the lungs – hence Felix's pneumonia. But, as the doctors kept telling us, even all together these symptoms told us very little: there could be a thousand reasons for any or all of them from benign to fatal, it was just too early to say. I remained resolutely upbeat, not so much in denial as disbelief. The babies having anything seriously wrong with them seemed so unlikely; I was still deeply convinced that these things only happened to other people.

A month after the birth I was struggling with breastfeeding. Because the boys were both being tube-fed, I was completely reliant on the electric breast pump, and this was bringing its own problems. Aside from the nipple soreness that a month of pumping had caused, it was incredibly hard to supply enough milk for two babies without any actual feeding. A mother produces milk in response to a number of factors, with suction being just one. Her baby's cry, and even the sight of him suckling, combine with a hormonal rush to set off the 'let-down reflex' and release the milk. Pumping at home, without the sensory stimulation of a baby, was bringing ever-diminishing returns and, inevitably, people around me were starting to suggest that maybe it was time to give up the idea of breastfeeding altogether.

I knew that it made sense in many ways: the health benefits to the boys were almost certainly not worth the misery it was causing me, but this was not only about what the babies needed. It was also true that providing breast milk was the one thing that I alone could do. It affirmed my status as their mother, a physical link between me and their well-being. They needed me and I, in return, needed them too. It was all too easy to feel that they weren't mine at all, but that they actually belonged to the hospital. So I brought in expensive French perfumery, baby soaps and colognes so that they would smell different from the other hospital babies, funky outfits from BabyGap, even though they never went anywhere and I gritted my teeth through the nightly pumping, so my boys could be breastfed. With these small acts, I was staking my claim, asserting my ownership of them, and telling myself that they really did belong with me and that, one day, they really would be with me.

The only thing about the babies that wasn't little and frail was their spirit. They were still only a month old and Theo had never left the NICU, but they were already making their very different personalities apparent. Felix was the feisty one, still a noticeable chunk smaller than his twin but stronger, crosser, braver and more sociable. Fee always wanted to see what was going on and would cry to be picked up and work himself into a fury when he was put down. Theo was an altogether more serene child. There was an aura of peacefulness around him that remained unruffled, even during the daily poking and prodding that would enrage Felix. Theo loved to be held, not so he could get a better view of the action, but just for the comfort of a cuddle. And he was filled with love, a real mummy's boy; when I was in the room he never took his eyes off me.

They really were cute together and I could watch them for hours. I found their physical ease with each other fascinating and I'm sure that, in those early days, they had little concept of themselves as two different people. Their tiny little fingers would intertwine or explore noses, mouths, eyes and clothes and, if not carefully watched, had a nice line in pulling out each other's feeding tubes which drove the nurses nuts, but never failed to make me laugh. Their physical similarity didn't end with their looks either. The nurses found that very often their hearts beat in unison and, most comically of all, they even seemed to poo within minutes of each other.

As the boys continued to improve, the fears about them gradually receded. They saw a speech therapist who looked at their suck/swallow/breathe coordination and pronounced them 'still pretty immature' but the general consensus from doctors, geneticists and assorted therapists seemed to be that there was nothing seriously wrong and that time and patience would cure everything. They moved into the low dependency unit, right beside the NICU front door, and Danny and I were flooded with relief. I could see the end of the nightmare at last; it felt as though we were through the worst of it.

The last stage before home is 'rooming in' which is when you are put in a little hospital bed-sit adjacent to the NICU and left to your own devices. You have no nurses around, you have to cope alone: it's a last practice-run in the security of the hospital before the safety net is truly taken away. Alone at last with my babies, I was nervous but happy. It didn't seem real; we were actually going to be allowed to go home all together. Their feeding tubes had been removed and I was even still breastfeeding, something I'd come so close to giving up. In the little fake home, I sat revelling in them both; even managing to get them both latched on to feed at the same time. Holding them in my arms, looking down on their beautiful little faces as they fed, I was filled with pride for all of us: me, them, Danny, even Evie and Joey. I felt like we'd climbed a mountain but now, after a hard and tortuous road to the top, we were finally about to start our new life as a family together. But, as I was to learn only too well, taking anything for granted is just asking for trouble.

We were supposed to room-in for forty-eight hours. Roughly halfway through the second day I noticed Theo was a little pale and quieter than usual; I alerted one of the doctors. Over the next hour we watched him go downhill rapidly. He was whisked back into intensive care and started immediately on a course of powerful antibiotics and, because his condition had deteriorated so rapidly and dramatically, he was given a blood transfusion. Within a few hours he had perked up enough to be moved back into the high dependency unit, where he remained, panic over, back in an incubator, drips, tubes and machines everywhere but looking more like himself again, whilst I wept tears of desperate frustration into Danny's shoulder. The doctors told me that they suspected an infection although, once again, they couldn't find anything definite. I was devastated: it felt particularly cruel for fate to play this card when I was so close to winning the game.

There was a good deal of crying that night as I railed against the whole situation and blew off some of the tension that had been building since the boys were born. For weeks I had been biting my tongue, trying to rise above the daily frustration and stay focused on getting my children home, but now I gave vent to my feelings, working my way through a box of Kleenex in a puddle of self-piteous misery.

Some recent research has found, as I've long suspected, that human tears actually contain many of the hormones and chemicals that are associated with depression and stress. A good cry is cleansing and calming, it washes out sadness and lightens the heavy heart. I cried out much of my fear and rage and, once calm, was ready to face reality again.

With Theo succumbing to *another* bug, the doctors naturally wanted to keep a very close eye on Felix for the next few days and this meant that, despite Felix being quite well, all thoughts of home were shelved for the time being. I felt like I'd been kicked in the guts and, after being able to pick Theo up and cuddle him whenever I wanted, seeing him back in an incubator and attached to monitors and drips was incredibly hard. As usual, I turned to my online friends to unload the confusion of my emotions.

'*Even after all these weeks we still have no real explanation for why the boys have been so ill. Almost full-term, good sizes – their behaviour has been a puzzle to everyone. They've had so many tests now and everything has come back negative. No genetic or chromosome disorders, no viruses found or bacterial cultures grown, all x-rays and ultrasounds normal. Has anyone else had this? I feel like I really need to know why they're so immature.*

My boys are so sweet and so beautiful and I JUST WANT THEM HOME WITH ME NOT STUCK IN THE STUPID HOSPITAL WHERE NO ONE CAN EVEN TELL ME WHAT'S WRONG WITH THEM.'

The following day things were looking up. Felix was still not showing any signs of catching the mystery bug that his brother had and Theo was looking more like his usual self. I, on the other hand, was feeling depressed and demoralised. The doctor had told me that Theo could be unhooked from his monitor for a while and I knew that a restorative cuddle would make us both feel better. He was already wide awake so I lifted him out of his cot, holding him close in my arms and talking to him. I told him what a fright he'd given me and how much I wanted him to come home; and then, out of the blue, *Theo William Shisler smiled at me*! Not an 'is that a smile or is it wind' smile, but a real, proper baby-face, gummy smile. I could barely contain my joy. Any mother will tell you that their baby's first smile is precious and beautiful, but this smile of Theo's was even more special. My boy was not quite six weeks old and here he was, smiling. Theo was smiling at five weeks old, just as Joey had and Evie had: he was developmentally right on target. Now I had proof that, whatever else was wrong, my little one was cognitively doing fine. I grinned back at him, smiling through tears now, joy-filled not just by the fact of his smile, but also by his exquisite timing: lifting me at the exact moment I was starting to lose hope. What a gift! Even the senior paediatrician was almost moved to tears, as my happy and exuberant relief rippled through the nursery.

As if to underline the positive mood, the doctor told me that as long as Felix stayed well over the next couple of days, and there was every reason to believe he would, he could come home without Theo. That night, as I made my daily report to the Twins List, it felt good to be able to share some happy news for a change:

> '*It's been a rough few days; I wanted to list some of the good moments... The first time I held both my babies together; seeing Felix with no tubes or monitors attached; breastfeeding Theo for the first time; sharing smiles with other mothers in the NICU; every ounce of weight gain; the babies' first bath time and the way they smelled afterwards;*

all the love I've received from this list...and Theo's first
smile today – just for me, just when I needed it most.'

And, for the first time in weeks, I slept soundly all night.

* * *

Bringing Felix home without Theo was bittersweet. It was wonderful to have him there and, with three of my four children at home, it felt like life was returning to something like an even keel. But I felt awful that Theo would now be all alone in the hospital and prayed that it wouldn't be for too long. Felix still seemed so very tiny and vulnerable, I barely dared leave him even to go to the toilet; I checked him constantly, with a level of anxiety that far outweighed anything I had felt with my other children.

Evie rose to the momentousness of the occasion by uttering her first sentence. Taking one look at the minuscule attention sponge that was her baby brother, she announced firmly, 'Mummy, no baby!' before making off with his dummy, blanket and socks. So much for sisterly love.

After almost six weeks of waiting, I finally got to use the double buggy I'd bought during my pregnancy. Felix was still too little and floppy to actually sit in the pram but, bundled up in blankets and propped with cushions, I was able to get him reasonably secure in the seat. Evie was strapped in beside him and then, with Joey on one arm and Danny on the other, we headed to the park. It was a beautiful late spring day and it was fantastic to be doing something purely for pleasure. I revelled in how 'ordinary' we looked, like every other family in the park enjoying the sunshine and, just for a little while, I let myself forget about the NICU, Theo and all the drama of the past few months.

> *'The boys will be six weeks old tomorrow. I feel like I want to grieve for this lost time but I daren't let myself go just yet, I might not be able to stop. Maybe when it's all over I can sort through what I'm feeling.'*

I felt like I'd been robbed of their first month: it was so unfair, my children's infancy was slipping away and I would never get this time back. Even though I knew that it was nothing, only a drop in the ocean compared to a whole lifetime we would have together, I felt desperately sad. Joey was already twelve, I knew how quickly the years passed, I didn't want to waste another second. I had to stop waiting for the twins to come home, putting all our lives on hold, and get on with trying to savour every moment of all their precious childhoods. OK, we didn't have Theo home but we did have Felix, perhaps I should be relishing this chance to settle them in one at a time – the glass didn't have to be half-empty, I just needed an adjustment of perspective. And then...

> *'I **hate** to be writing this. Thirty-six hours after being discharged from hospital, Felix was readmitted this morning and is now back in an incubator in the high dependency unit. He began choking and started to have difficulties with his breathing again. By the time Danny got him to the hospital he was blue and limp. He's OK now but we were*

very frightened. The hospital will start a new lot of tests tomorrow when he has had a chance to rest for a bit and recover from his shock.

*Walking out of the hospital with his empty car seat **again**, coming home to all his stuff lying around **again**, all these reminders that our babies are not here. I feel very close to breaking today. Danny and I continue to put one foot in front of the other because what else is there to do? In any case the children all need us to be strong. The hospital has told us to prepare ourselves for a long haul – they are as baffled as ever.*

I'm so scared and so tired and I'm starting to be afraid to have hope because every time I do, something like this happens. I wish I knew how to stay positive.'

It had been a very close run thing with Felix that morning; terrifying for Danny, he got Felix to hospital in the nick of time. We sat in miserable silence as a clearly shaken doctor told us that, if we *ever* found ourselves with a child struggling to breathe again, we should call an ambulance rather than relying on the god of traffic jams to whisk us through the rush-hour streets. No one could tell us anything except that this was a long way from being resolved: we would be hanging around the hospital for a good while yet.

I was exhausted, mentally, physically and emotionally. I could feel myself being crushed under the weight of anxiety and disappointment. Now it was me crying silent tears, bewildered and demoralised but, more than anything, exhausted. I wanted to walk away. I didn't want to be Pollyanna-Supermummy any more; I just wanted my life back. It had only been six weeks since the boys were born, but it felt so much longer. It wasn't the time that was grinding me down, it was the heartbreak of having my hopes repeatedly built up, only to be unceremoniously ripped away time and time again. To add insult to injury, I was increasingly aware that it was not only Theo and Felix who were missing a mother: my daily vigil at the hospital meant that Evie and Joey had barely seen me as well. And, at the bottom of my huge pile of woes, sat the unspoken fear that this was just the beginning, there was a lot worse to come.

~ 9 ~

When I look back on this period of my life, it's hard to get a clear view. There was so much drama, so many false dawns and disappointments, theories, plans, projections and possibilities; days and even months blur into each other. What I do remember is how it felt, and how we learned to survive in the chaos. I remember that just 'being OK' took a massive, almost superhuman, effort. When you are all adrift in uncharted waters, when there is nowhere to anchor yourself, nothing solid to cling to and no signs of hopeful land on the horizon, a successful day is simply one where you don't drown. I can retrace my steps through the letters I wrote, daily updates to friends and strangers, a continuous line of thoughts, feelings and events that brought a sense of order to an increasingly disordered life. The letters saved me more than once; writing them brought clarity and focus and, of course, the replies brought comfort beyond measure. And I remember my babies, and falling in love with them a little more each day. Two little conundrums, a seemingly endless list of quirks and questions, all wrapped up in cuteness and charm.

* * *

With Felix readmitted, Danny and I desperate and demoralised and both boys remaining frustratingly enigmatic, it was time to regroup. It took a day or so to shake off the misery and disappointment that felt like it had seeped right into my bones, but there was no choice but to pick myself up and get on with it; falling apart was not an option. There were new worries now as well. The NICU policy was to handle the babies as little as possible and, while this was fine for the majority of impossibly fragile NICU patients, Felix and Theo were now six weeks old and starting to take an active interest in the world around them. There was precious little entertainment for them where they were. They loved being picked up and played with, or held so that they could see the action in the unit, but even putting a baby seat, let alone bringing any toys, into this rigidly controlled environment was impossible. It was also abundantly clear that the neonatalist doctors were coming to the end of their ability to treat or even diagnose my boys, so it was no great surprise to find their consultant waiting for me when I arrived one morning, in order to tell me that we would be 'graduating' to a regular paediatric ward in another part of the hospital.

I had mixed feelings about the move. Despite all the excellent reasons for getting out of the NICU, it had become a familiar place and, in this period of ultra-uncertainty, familiarity was not something to be easily tossed away.

Galaxy, the general paediatric ward in University College

Hospital, was in the main building, and linked to the maternity hospital/NICU via a long, bizarre underground tunnel system that also connected to the chapel, the medical school, the nurses' accommodation, some research labs and the morgue. Not generally seen by the public, who would be directed to the regular, street-level route, it was a dank and unlovely place that smelt of death, urine and hospital food, and bore signs of sneaky and defiantly unhealthy cigarette smoking by every single one of its doors to the real world. Felix and Theo were trundled through the tunnel in their little plastic cots, saucer-eyed with excitement, taking in every second of this new experience.

Galaxy Ward was situated at the top of the building, on the sixth floor. From our room we had a view right across central London. The spring sunshine streamed across the beds and the chatter of children could be heard coming from the playroom across the hall. The contrast between this lively and child-centred place and the dimly lit hush of the NICU was huge; I thought about how easy it would be to bring Evie here when I visited. I felt positive and optimistic: at least something was happening now. I hoped it wouldn't be too long before we got to the bottom of the problem and were able to start getting them better. We *could* do this; it *was* going to be OK. I was given a couple of questionnaires to complete about the boys' likes, dislikes and routines. It felt strange to be answering questions about their bedtimes and bath routine; until this point I had never been asked to make decisions for them: we did what we were told in the NICU, where even the smallest actions were regulated by the doctors' edicts. Now, finally, I was being treated as a mother. For the first time I had a sense that they were my children and that, actually, I knew what was best for them.

I was excited by this new-found responsibility and thrilled with the huge change in my status, reeling off a list of dos and don'ts about bedtimes, bath routines and clothing for the nursing notes. My impotence on the NICU had been horribly frustrating, but I consoled myself with the thought that at least this experience should make me a better mother. I would no longer take for granted the rights and privileges of parenthood, but would appreciate the precious gifts they were. After six weeks of playing second fiddle to medical protocol – as well as having Joey and Evie both being cared for by other people, albeit at home – I had lost sight of the fact that I was actually a pretty decent mother. I had four children now, plus more than a decade of child-rearing experience and, demonstrably more accurate than any medical monitoring, I had my maternal intuition. A mother's instinct is an incredible thing. It's there from the first baby's first heartbeat, and yet I was only just becoming aware of its extraordinarily sophisticated and sensitive power, more than twelve years after it first raised its niggling cry. When I was a new, first-time mother to Joey all those years ago, older, wiser women would tell me to trust my instinct, to listen to my heart because a mother always knew what was best for her own child. And I would try, *really* try. I would strain to pick out the sound of my own intuition from the huge number of advisory words that rattled through my panicky young head. It was, of course, impossible. Between the conflicting rules on feeding, nappies, dummies and the rest; between the myriad sources of friends and family, magazines and midwives, I heard nothing except my own rising terror. It drove me nuts. 'Trust yourself' they would say and I would think '*but how do I know which voice is mine?*' Now, though, I knew the sound of my own voice and I knew how to listen to it. After twelve years, it was strong enough and clear enough to even rise above the words of the supposed experts: the doctors. It was always me who saw that, for instance, one of the boys was getting sick, hours before anything would register on one of the monitors. Now, with the stakes so high and my sons' well-being so precariously balanced, that nagging voice had become a roar; and I had learned to be a lioness.

University College Hospital may be a world-renowned institution, with a highly regarded medical school and a cutting-edge research department, but as a casual visitor, you would never guess as much. To get to the paediatric Galaxy ward you have to first fight your way through the delightful accident and emergency department. This is London's most central hospital, sitting at the unlovely end of Tottenham Court Road and just a few minutes' walk from Euston and King's Cross stations. It is a magnet for every alcoholic and junkie in the area, and this is an area not short of either. Add to this the fallout from the West End party crowd, the increasing numbers of mentally ill 'care in the community' refugees plus your regular head-in-a-bucket kids' accidents and you have a recipe for grimness and menacing despair that is second to none. It did, however, look a lot worse than it was and, though often intimidated, I soon found I could slip through the forlorn and fractured crowds without attracting any unwanted attention.

The medical plan for Felix and Theo, once we arrived on Galaxy, was still pretty sketchy, but essentially we would continue trying to identify the reasons for their ongoing failure to thrive, whilst trying to get them strong and stable enough to go home. Their repeated chest infections and endless problems with feeding had led the doctors to suggest a barium swallow test (a kind of moving x-ray) which would let us watch the progress of food from mouth to stomach; they were booked in for the test the following morning and I arrived at the hospital bright and early, ready to accompany them to x-ray.

'*Halfway down the corridor I realised that Felix was looking a bit off-colour and so we decided not to risk it and just send Theo for the test. I stayed with Felix on the ward. All his observations were completely normal (heart rate, respiratory rate, temp, saturations) but, once again, maternal instinct proves more accurate than modern technology. Within an hour he was having one of his "episodes". Choking, going blue, tons of mucus collecting in his throat – luckily this time we were in the hospital and the doctors were able to see the whole thing and get oxygen to him straight away. I just found myself standing there saying, "I knew he was sick, I knew he was sick," over and over, like that was going to help! They're both back on tube feeding only.*

Meanwhile, Theo had the barium swallow and, of course, it didn't really tell us anything we hadn't already guessed. He is inhaling a little of his feed and his swallow/

suck is "discordant" (i.e. he can't do it). We assume the
same is true for Felix. What we still don't know is why. I'm
going nuts here, I didn't realise that I'd placed so much
hope in getting some answers today. I still am no nearer to
knowing if this is going to take weeks, months or even
years to put right. Actually, I don't know if it can ever be
put right. The doctors are now talking about doing a
biopsy of their muscle tissue – I feel punch drunk and
weary beyond belief.

Sometimes I am scared they might not make it at
all. Today has been a bit like that. Theo seems fine today
*but Felix looks really ill again. If I only **knew** what to*
expect, I'm sure I could handle it better, this uncertainty is
really tough.'

As a teenager I had a reputation among my friends of being a bit
of a drama queen. I don't know how fair an assessment this was
(there was, after all, a considerable amount of very real and
traumatic drama in my teenage life) but, nevertheless, I took the
accusation hard and, ever since, have resolutely down-played
major events in my life. As the situation with Theo and Felix
became increasingly serious, and even as I was sharing the full
drama of it with my online community, I was still listening to the
voice in my head that was telling me I was being unnecessarily
melodramatic. I think that, even by this point, I was still gripped
by the conviction that these things always happened to someone
else. The idea of profound disability was still so utterly foreign to
me that, although I was writing about it and knew intellectually

that it was a very real possibility, in my heart I simply did not believe it. How does this deep-seated denial square with the reawakening of my super-sensitive maternal instinct? I don't know, but it did. Somewhere in the flurry of fear and intense emotions, the line between what I knew and didn't know became a blur of contradictions where I was able to see everything, and nothing, all at the same time.

I'd been to get a sandwich, leaving the twins asleep together. They were unbelievably cute, curled together into a single ball of tiny hands and feet and soft little heads. It was a lovely day and I'd regained my equilibrium after the barium swallow bad news; so when I arrived back on the ward to find the consultant waiting for me and the curtains drawn around the bed, I didn't immediately click that this was 'an event'. Now, of course, I am well-versed in the ways of doctors and I can smell bad news the second it enters my orbit. But back then, in those early days, I didn't recognise the signs.

The consultant had managed to find a couple of chairs for us (nowadays this would make my internal alarm *scream*) and she gestured me to sit down. She looked me directly in the eye as she spoke, her words were slow and deliberate, and I remember wondering if she'd been trained to do that, to ensure that I heard and understood. It was the worst possible news: I was being told that, more than likely, the babies would not 'just grow out of' whatever it was that they had. She pointed out several things about them (their lack of clear facial expressions, their permanently open mouths and their posture while sleeping) which were indicators of a congenital neuromuscular disorder. She said she wanted to begin a whole battery of testing in order to try and discover exactly which disorder it was.

I couldn't speak. I think I mumbled something about was she sure? I remember her saying to me, 'I know you want to ask me about life expectancy,' and thinking 'Well, I do *now*!' Because, until that moment it had never occurred to me to ask something so very serious. And then I was half-hearing her and half-realising that it *was* serious, it really was. It was as serious as it could be and it was real. And it was happening to me!

The rest of the conversation (if you can call something so one-sided a conversation) is a bit of a blur, to be honest. The doctor told me that there was a huge variation in things that could be causing the babies' problems, and also a huge variation in the severity of these disorders. Some, she told me, were milder and would allow Theo and Felix to lead a relatively normal life with a full lifespan. In other cases the babies would be very profoundly disabled both mentally and physically. In the very worst case, they would not survive infancy.

I had to get out of the hospital; to get away from the ward, from the doctor and her terrible words. My body was numb and I felt as though I had been dropped into a glass jar; everything around me seemed muffled and distorted. I think I said I needed to get something and then bolted from the ward, running down the six flights of stairs, through the Hieronymus Bosch landscape of A and E and out on to the street. As the fresh air hit me, I realised that I had no idea where I was going; I just needed a few minutes of empty space in order to absorb this information. I walked to a local shop and bought a newspaper, and then I went back to the ward and my babies. Danny was arriving from home just as I walked into Felix and Theo's room. Now I was able to listen properly as the doctor relayed her thinking and tentative diagnosis to my husband. Hearing it all again didn't seem to make it any more real: this woman was telling me that my babies might die and it was just completely and utterly beyond my comprehension. I looked over at Danny's drawn and grey face and realised that I probably looked the same; we looked beyond exhausted, sick with worry.

At home, as I wrote my update to the List, my emotions finally managed to cut through the thick blanket of numbness I'd wrapped myself in.

'To me, of course, they are still perfect in every way; I love them desperately and am finding it very hard to believe that this is happening. When you hear a doctor say those words to you a big part of your brain just shuts down.

Today has been so very hard. Breaking the news to my mum, seeing the double buggy sitting in my hallway and wondering if I'll ever get to use it. How will this affect my other kids? I've tried to explain to Joey as calmly and gently as I can. Oh God, this is killing me; I really didn't know that anything could hurt this much.'

By the time I clicked send, I could barely see the screen through my tears. My relationship with my list-mates had become increasingly intimate as the weeks passed; these strangers were being told things that even those closest to me didn't know. For my family and friends, and even for the medical staff who were an increasingly dominant presence in my world, I was trying so hard to keep positive, fully focused on creating an environment of hope that would be conducive to getting the babies home. But online I could drop all the faux-cheeriness and honestly open my heart. I voiced my worst fears, railed against doctors and even found space to laugh at myself and the absurdity of my new life. The Twins List provided me with a much-needed safety valve, a place to unload all my negativity at the end of each day. Just as important as the cathartic experience of writing was the unconditional love and support I got in return. Every morning I would wake to a new batch of emails letting me know that I was doing a good job, that one day this really would be behind us, that we could do it. Just the fact of knowing that so many people, all around the world, were following our journey, praying for our family, just *caring* about us, made a difference, made it easier: I was not alone.

Despite the grimness of the consultant's opinion there was, at least for Danny, some good that came out of her talk. Armed now with a few scraps of information, some new medical terms and a more complete picture of the boys' problems, he was at last able to hit the internet and do some research. He'd really struggled with the impotence of not being able to help, but online research was his forte: if there was any more information out there, he would get it. It didn't take him long to find the website of a speech therapist who specialised in feeding issues and had developed a ground-breaking form of treatment as well as a range of oral strengthening and stimulation aids. Danny was ecstatic: this looked perfect for the twins, we could hardly wait to get to the hospital and share our findings with Felix and Theo's medical team. For Danny, being able to do something practical for his sons was hugely significant. I had given breast milk, spending weeks hooked up to the monstrous milking machine, but Danny felt as though he had been able to do nothing but visit. Now he was actually helping, finding, at last, a role for himself in this medical pantomime.

Danny virtually dragged me to the hospital the following morning, desperate to share the fruits of his labour. We saw the speech therapist first; she'd heard of the woman Danny had found and agreed that some of her therapy ideas would be very useful for Felix and Theo. During the ward rounds, Danny gave copies of his printouts to the consultant as she came into our room. Her reaction seemed dismissive. She briefly glanced at the papers she'd been given, telling Danny and me: 'Stay away from the internet, you're just setting yourselves up for heart-break.' She then went on to outline her views on the subject of parental research: there was a huge amount of information out there, and we had no way of distinguishing between 'good' (i.e. academic) and 'bad' ('someone's granny in a shed at the bottom of the garden'), so we should leave it to the experts. In any case, she told us, they had internet access in the hospital; if there was useful information out there, they'd find it themselves.

Danny was gutted. I think this was the beginning of the shift in our attitude to doctors. Up until now we had, like most people, placed them on pedestals, revered their opinions and trusted their views. This, though: this was absurd! Did she really think that we, as parents, would *not* try to find as much information about our own children as possible? Did she really think we were so stupid that we would believe any old rubbish we read without checking and double checking? For Danny and I, this was a turning point in our relationship with the medical experts: her dismissal of our internet research was, for us, like a spotlight on the medical profession's limitations. So far on this bizarre journey, the *only* thing that had been consistently reliable was *my* maternal intuition.

Our new understanding of the fallibility and limitations of medical professionals was to serve us well over the next few months, when we would hear more opinions and prognoses than we had ever thought possible. The truth was, in the strange world of medically rare conditions, we were as good at being experts as anyone, and hardly any less likely to stumble across answers during our ignorant web-surfing, as they were with their ever-so-slightly-better-informed trawl. Plus we had parental passion on our side – the very best motivator.

Having made her ballpark diagnosis of a neuromuscular disorder, the consultant decided to send the boys somewhere they could be properly tested, in the hopes of narrowing down the field of possible diseases. If we knew exactly what was wrong with them, we could start to make plans for their future: if they had one. Even if the news was very bleak and the boys had some terrible degenerating condition, we could at least make the time we had with them as joyful as possible. We were to be referred to the neurology department of Great Ormond Street Hospital (GOSH), where Felix and Theo would go through state-of-the-art testing for dozens of syndromes, conditions and diseases, and would be seen by some of the country's finest paediatric neurologists. Great Ormond Street: the world-famous children's hospital, the recipient of all royalties from J.M. Barrie's *Peter Pan*, national institution and the last hope of desperate parents everywhere. *Thank God!*

Great Ormond Street holds a very particular place in the psyche of the British public. Through its massive fundraising effort, The Wishing Well Appeal, to rebuild the crumbling original hospital, and its close ties with its patron, the late Princess Diana, GOSH has generated more public awareness than any other hospital in the UK. It's a source of huge national pride and there have been countless stories of medical miracles over the years. And not just miracles, but miracles for children, so much more moving than adults, with their innocence, their absolute blamelessness and their *whole lives* ahead of them. The rebuilding appeal was a huge success; money poured in to GOSH from, seemingly, every inch of the country. There were vast, nationwide fundraising events; noble efforts made by schools and scout troops; pocket money donated by tiny children. Everyone gave, everyone got involved and, more than any institution I can think of, GOSH belongs to the British people. You see evidence of this ownership everywhere in the hospital. Above every door, in every lift, and even on the side of each large piece of equipment there is an engraved plaque that tells you where the relevant money came from – 'The People of Lancashire'; 'The family and friends of Jack Smith (age 8), RIP'; 'The Third Fulham Brownie Pack'. Great Ormond Street Hospital is a national treasure, it's the perfect combination of cutting-edge science and family-friendly compassion; and now we were going to be part of the magic.

For the third time in less than two months, Danny and I had another whole new world to get our heads around. Great Ormond Street is utterly unlike the average NHS hospital; it is bright and airy, designed with its tiny patients in mind, and clearly not cash-starved like most hospitals. The building itself is still quite new with dozens of thoughtful touches that make the hospital experience a little less forbidding for children. There are toys everywhere: a big playbus is the first thing you see as you walk in. There are stars on the ceilings of the lifts, presumably to soothe little nerves as they are wheeled to the operating theatre. Walls are cheerfully bright, wooden aeroplanes are suspended from the ceiling; dustbins are giant frogs, catching litter in their comically gaping mouths. Even the name tags worn by the staff are decorated with stars and stickers, while wards are named after woodland creatures and other whimsical themes. There are no visiting hours here, parents are encouraged to stay with their children and each ward has a kitchenette where mums and dads can make tea.

But look a little closer. Beneath the gloss and kid-friendly fun, the reality of GOSH is very different. The lightest scratch of the surface brings the truth into focus: this is a place dealing with very sick children. Children who have exhausted the skills or knowledge of their local hospital, children who may be hanging on to life by a thread. Everywhere you look there is another child bearing some seemingly unbearable load. Terrible deformities, swollen and sore bodies, the hairless pale heads of the cancer children; so much devastating illness it is overwhelming at first. Then there are the parents: grey-faced, sleep-deprived eyes that are swollen and red from crying, exhausted bodies, shoulders rigid with anxiety.

I recognised myself in them and was bizarrely comforted; here we were just another family in crisis, one of many, not some unlikely victims of freakishly bad luck. Here, among all this fear and uncertainty, we were finally 'normal'. And, like every other family arriving at GOSH, we were filled with hope and expectation. Now we would get our answers, now we would unravel the mystery of our babies' health; in this legendary place, all our questions would be answered. Rationally I suppose I knew that a 'cure' was unlikely but, then again, this was the home of miracles, so I allowed a secret hope to bed down in my heart because 'you never know' and because, if this was at all fixable, then this was the place to fix it.

Once we were settled on the neurophysiology ward, our new doctors arrived for their first good look at the babies. This time I had braced myself: I wouldn't be caught off-guard by a doctor again. I was ready for bad news, though still praying that it would be tempered by hope. We didn't need much either, even the smallest sliver would be enough to ease our journey through these difficult times. I have found that, in general, doctors tend to give the bleakest prognosis to their patients, as though denial is some terrible, life-threatening disease that must be eradicated at all costs. They tell you the very worst that can happen in order, I suppose, to prevent future heartache. But, for parents of sick children, hope is our lifeblood, we need to believe all will be well, we need to stay focused on positivity, and sometimes denial is the only thing that stands between us and paralysing fear and grief. This time we were in luck.

> '*The doctor says that their general tone is not too bad and that she feels that their problem is concentrated around the jaw/tongue/throat (they have almost no ability to suck and they rarely swallow). Whilst she is not ruling out any of the more serious outcomes at this stage (life-threatening conditions or major disability) she believes that we have reasonable grounds to hope for better, maybe much better. To my question, "Is it possible that this could completely resolve itself in time?" she replied, "It's not **impossible**".*'

It's not *impossible*. There it was: hope. Those three words were enough for Danny and me, enough for us to erase the previous prognosis. We were in Great Ormond Street now; as far as we were concerned these people were the ultimate experts, and we instinctively trusted them. Of course, it was all only words at this stage; the tests would be started the following morning. More poking and prodding for my poor babies but, I hoped, it would be the last for them. If we actually got some answers, it would all have been worthwhile.

Great Ormond Street is actually situated in one of the most charming parts of central London. Bloomsbury has a long charitable, literary and bohemian tradition; Charles Dickens lived a few streets away, as did T.S. Eliot. Sir Thomas Coram, the eighteenth-century philanthropist who opened the original Foundlings Hospital (as GOSH was first known), centred all his good works here; Virginia Wolfe's coterie of writers and artists even took their name from the area (the famous Bloomsbury Set). Today Coram's Fields still exists as a safe playspace for local children, and the pretty streets and delightful leafy squares around the hospital still contain a mixture of quirky shops, elegant restaurants and imposing London town houses. Having settled Felix and Theo in to their new surroundings, Danny and I decided to take advantage of our newly optimistic mood; we booked a babysitter for Evie and Joey, and headed out into the lovely, early summer evening.

I have always enjoyed walking through London, and one of the best things about living centrally is that you rarely need to use a car. Danny and I strolled arm-in-arm through the streets looking for somewhere to eat and enjoying the mild weather. It was good just doing something nice together; focusing, even briefly, on ourselves. Over dinner we chatted about everything, from our deepest fears for our children to the previous night's television. I was so grateful for the solid bedrock of my marriage: that alone made everything more manageable. We had been through so much together, and I felt as bonded to my husband as I did to my own shadow. Through everything that had happened, he had never wavered from my side, not for a single second, whether it was holding hands through anxious moments, or gossiping about the family in the next room. Danny is, without doubt, the love of my life but, more importantly, he is my best friend. After dinner we walked home feeling sleepy but upbeat: tomorrow would be a big day with all the babies' testing kicking off. I was glad I'd had the chance to de-stress a bit in preparation. Despite my anxiety about the testing, and what it might reveal, I was glad we were finally doing *something*.

'Well after all the hoo-ha build up, we actually got off to a pretty slow start on the testing today. The hospital got some emergency admissions so Felix and Theo got bumped from their morning slot and didn't go for their MRI scans until 5.30. In the end they could only do Theo as Felix was too wriggly. I don't have the results yet but the nurse who went with them told me that she didn't hear anyone say anything terrible... The main consultant ward rounds are tomorrow morning so it'll be interesting to hear the expert's thoughts on the boys. Hopefully the EMG's will be done tomorrow (as well as Felix's scan) but I have learned not to expect anything.

I'm feeling pretty emotional tonight. My darling boys are almost two months old and I still don't have any idea when they'll be home. It could be many months and I miss them so much. My heart breaks every time I walk out of that hospital without them; this isn't the way it's supposed to be. While I was pregnant Danny and I bought the biggest bed we could find. We figured we'd need it to fit all those kids in for our family cuddles at the weekends. It doesn't seem like a lot to ask for and yet it seems a million miles away. All the uncertainty is really tough, I don't know what I dare hope for— I don't even know for sure that we'll ever all be together. I try to stay focused on today instead of looking ahead but sometimes today, where I'm separated from my children, is a hard place to be and then I want to look to the future and I can't...

*Mostly though I **am** OK. Sometimes I'm even happy. Whatever happens, this has changed me. It's a cliché I know, but I sure have got my priorities figured out now. I used to think that somewhere inside me there was a need for some big "achievement", now I know that I will die happy if I can just raise four happy kids who are loved and secure and be a good and loving partner to Danny. I know it sounds pretty lame but I swear it's true. I only wish it hadn't taken something like this to help me figure out what's really important in life. Funnily enough, I think I will find it a lot easier to be happy in the future, I am learning to appreciate life's gifts so much more.'*

The results from the tests were not at all what we expected. The muscle function tests had, incredibly, come back normal, as had their hearing and vision tests. It was their brain scans that were causing the most concern. The doctor explained to Danny and me that there were some very slight abnormalities: tiny spots of calcium and a little less myelin (a substance found in the brain which helps conduct messages) than was usual. What it meant was still impossible to discern. We discovered that neurology is still a pretty inexact science; the human brain remains largely mysterious, and these small findings could indicate massive and profound disability, or something quite unremarkable. We were told that we probably would never get a clear diagnosis or a name for their problem. Most of these things were so rare, they were as good as unique. A further test, a muscle biopsy to check the actual structure of the muscles, had been cancelled. The doctor told us that as the muscle function test was normal, there was no reason to expect anything to come from the biopsy. In addition to this, a biopsy was a painful and intrusive test, to be done only when absolutely necessary. The doctor was clear, the problem was not with their muscles, it was in their brains. The messages from brain to muscle, the ones that controlled movement, were not getting through properly.

Hindsight can be a terrible thing; a curse that gnaws at your peace of mind. We would later discover that the babies had a rare condition that could *only* be identified by muscle biopsy, regardless of muscle function tests. The tiny abnormalities on their brain scans were meaningless, a total red herring, they were neurologically fine. We were setting off down the wrong path, in the opposite direction from where we really needed to be.

We had also been told that a myelin deficiency, however slight, would generally indicate some level of learning disability. I, however, was certain that Felix and Theo were smart little buttons. Even though they were still only a couple of months old and, clearly, were not hitting any of their expected physical milestones, one look into their eyes and you could see their intelligence; to me it was obvious that there was nothing wrong with their cognitive functioning. The doctor looked at me indulgently as I told her that they were sharp as blades. I could see that, to her, it was just maternal pride that was stopping me from seeing the truth; but I knew I was right.

Of course, just to add to the general air of despondency, the babies got sick again. We were starting to see a pattern; hopes built up to be shattered again. One step forward, two back if we were lucky, otherwise it'd be three steps back, or more. Hanging on to even a shred of optimism was getting tougher by the day.

Felix had a couple of aspirations in the space of a few days which, combined with a virus that was floating around the hospital, made him really quite ill. Theo was also more congested than usual but, on this occasion, it was Felix who was the hardest hit. Once again I watched one of my babies go rapidly downhill until, inevitably, Felix was readmitted to intensive care. Within hours he was back on a ventilator, back on an antibiotic drip, off feeds again, blah, blah, blah… It was almost unbearable for me to see him back in the paediatric intensive care unit: he'd been through so much already in his short little life, I wanted to scream with anger and frustration at yet another big step backwards. Seeing my poor babies so miserable again, and feeling so utterly helpless to make them better, was suddenly overwhelming. I was so tired. The boys had just turned two months and the drama just felt relentless. The pain of being apart from them wasn't getting any easier to bear. I was just learning to live with it but, even so, I spent a sizeable portion of each day in tears. Even thinking positively was starting to feel like a risk: the comedown and inevitable disappointment was so painful. I forced myself to keep faith that we would, ultimately, get our happy ending. I could not afford to fall apart. Each morning I would walk to the hospital, willing there to be some better news on my arrival.

Better news was not forthcoming. As if to hammer home the reality of the situation, our next talk with the doctor was the bleakest so far. Despite the lack of a real diagnosis, she felt able to outline some probabilities about our future with our sons. In view of the fact that their problem was neurological rather than muscular (and the doctor said she was as convinced as she could be that this was the case), and as their current problems would have to be considered severe, we would have to expect that their future disabilities would also be serious. It was highly unlikely, we were told, that their feeding problems would ever resolve. Her immediate recommendation was that the boys should have surgery to place a permanent feeding tube, directly into their tummies: a gastrostomy. This, she believed, would protect them from the continual aspirations that were making them so ill. By putting the tube in, and also sealing the valve at the top of their stomachs, we would ensure that no milk, even just as reflux, could end up in their lungs. It made perfect sense, of course, but it was a huge leap for Danny and me. Surgery: it was so permanent. It meant a real, concrete acceptance of their disability and, of course, it meant putting our tiny, vulnerable babies through the upset and risk of an operation. I felt sick at the thought of causing them any more pain, but it was obvious that they were struggling to get through each day. I knew they could not get strong until we could get some decent nutrition into them and that was proving impossible. We asked for time to think about it, but it was really just time to absorb and accept: we knew that we would give our consent to the surgery; it was the only reasonable solution.

I think something changed in me about here. Until this point we had been living on our nerves, struggling to stay on top of a situation that was becoming more and more complex by the day. Our thoughts and plans had never changed: get the babies well and home as soon as possible, and then get on with our life. As the neurology results from GOSH plunged us further into uncertainty, I began to realise that I was going to have to find another way of coping. The principles of the twelve-step programme came back to me: acceptance of powerlessness; taking one day at a time; looking after my physical needs (not getting too hungry, angry, lonely or tired – things which act like a magnifier for emotions); faith in a power greater than myself; and trust that I would be given all I needed to cope with whatever life threw at me.

If addiction is about trying to escape from reality, then recovery is about learning to face reality without fear. The same tools that had carried me through my early months without alcohol would help me to navigate a path through these rocky times. This change in approach was reflected in my letters to the Twins List as I tried to fix my gaze resolutely on the bigger picture. Some of the Twins List families were starting to express dismay that, despite what must have been hundreds of hours of prayer said for the boys, from all around the world, Felix and Theo remained sick and in hospital. For me, though, this had now become a spiritual journey:

'Over the past two months I know that many of you have been praying/sending positive thoughts for my family. Well, you should all know that it has been working beautifully. Every day our boys bring us more joy and more love. We have found strengths within ourselves that we never knew existed and we are truly grateful for everything we have. We have been given an amazing gift in Felix and Theo, and a rare one. I cannot explain how *completely and utterly in love with them I am, they really are special and magical.*

*An experience such as this changes you on a very deep level; for me the change has been a positive one. I believe my heart is more open to the good things around me. I see just how many blessings I really have (top of the list – my **four** wonderful children). I **hate** being separated from Felix and Theo and am **desperate** to get them home from the hospital and it is **dreadful** seeing them suffer through all the tests but...I know that they are completely perfect and I **WOULD NOT CHANGE ONE SINGLE HAIR ON THEIR HEADS**.*

*Do not feel sorry for us, we are not "putting a brave face on it" and if you could see them you would know that this is true. We are luckier than most, we get to know these angels and keep them **forever**.'*

When I read these letters back now, I find them almost nauseatingly positive; the truth is I needed a strategy to get through a period that was harder than anything else I had ever done in my life. I was relentless in my search for good things to focus on: no blessing, however small, was deemed unworthy of celebrating. And it was true, I *did* have faith that, ultimately, things would turn out OK. I may not have known how the future would unfold, but I was sure that, whatever happened, we could still be a happy family. Theo and Felix were remarkable children who had already touched many lives and I was incredibly proud of them. It seemed to me that they had been sent to my family for a reason and, though I had no idea what that reason might be, I felt honoured to have been 'chosen'.

There were other AA skills that I called on to help me get through the most trying times: in recovery I had learned to 'act as if'. It's a clever and effective trick and it works well. If you are struggling with something (commonly faith in God) you 'act as if' you believe, change your behaviour, responses, attitudes, and your intellect will follow. By wearing the garb of someone whose life was filled with blessings and immeasurably enriched, I gradually became someone for whom that was true. It was crucial that I remained strong and positive. My children needed me to be able to cope, my husband needed me, so holding myself and my family in the light became a priority. This is not to say that I was never sad or upset, of course I was. But I also put huge effort into staying on track. Dark thoughts would be stamped on, not indulged; self-pity was a luxury I could not afford, because who could say where it might end? It was exhausting at times, and there were many, many days when I had to force myself to smile just to stop myself from screaming, but mostly it worked.

Part of the difficulty Danny and I were having in maintaining our equilibrium was that we were getting different prognoses from every doctor we saw, and sometimes even from the same doctor. The neurologist who had given us such bleak news just a week earlier, after then seeing a bright and chirpy Theo giggling and playing on the bed a few days later, revised her view and told me that perhaps their disabilities would be milder, maybe much milder, than she had previously thought. We saw another neurologist too. Like any parent on being given the other, more devastating news, we had asked for a second opinion. When it came it was, of course, very different suggesting that, by age ten, the twins might 'be a bit wobbly on their legs with poor speech' but would otherwise be normal. It was head-spinning. Eventually, after weeks of bouncing from one opinion to another, and the commensurate emotional ping-pong that went with it, I learned to rise above it and to keep a generous pinch of salt in my pocket at all times. We had by now been told at various times that the babies were immature, or they were fine, or severely disabled, or perhaps going to die, or brain damaged, or maybe just mildly disabled... They were Felix and Theo Shisler, our beautiful idiosyncratic sons, and that was really all we needed to know.

~ 10 ~

No matter how rough the days sometimes were, no matter how deeply into uncertainty we plunged, there was always something we could find to use as a light in the gloom. Felix and Theo themselves were breathtakingly lovely and as laden with character as they were bereft of strength. Their own relationship was astonishing and wonderful, filled with a love and care I never knew was possible in such tiny babies. Perhaps it was the grimness of their situation, the absence of home comforts and the lack of that constant parental presence that most infants have that bonded them together so tightly. Or maybe it was the fact that they were carved from the same stone, two identical buttons springing into life together. Whatever the cause, their delight in each other was infectious, and they would soothe and stroke and snuggle together, sleep wrapped in each other's arms and would fret at separation, snuffling and kissing when reunited and sucking each other's little thumbs.

As each day took us another step off the beaten track and further into unfamiliar territory, my daily updates to the Twins List started to take on an almost soap-operatic role. Each thrilling instalment seemed to end with a dramatic cliffhanger or an unlikely plot turn. I can barely imagine what it must have been like for those following our story but I did start to worry that our run of bad luck was so unlikely-sounding that people would surely soon start thinking that I was some terrible disturbed internet fantasist, making up tragic tales for attention or, worse still, with criminal intent. I had already been offered money by a couple of families (unfamiliar with the workings of British healthcare) and could easily have been setting up an elaborate sting, ready to fleece the kind and the gullible before vanishing into the ether. So, when I received an email from one of the other mothers on the list, telling me she was coming to London and would like to meet up, I was initially relieved that I would have a chance to prove things were really as I had portrayed them.

Tracy, a mother of four from South Carolina, would be my first 'in the flesh' contact with the list. It turned out she was a flight attendant with Delta Airlines and had been assigned to one of the regular London routes. She was going to be flying into Gatwick roughly once a month for the foreseeable future, a fact that made me quite nervous. I'm not, as I have mentioned, the most sociable person in the world and I can actually be, by turns, cripplingly shy and miserably misanthropic. One of the reasons I loved the Twins List was that I am so much more comfortable with the written rather than spoken word. The distance that stood between me and the other listees had, paradoxically, made me feel safe enough to open up much more than I would have under normal circumstances; I felt protected by this anonymity and so had developed a level of intimacy with the group that I would generally find oppressive. Now I was going to actually meet one of the people to whom I had poured out my heart and I had a horrible sinking feeling that, not only would we not get on, but we would be forced into fake amity once a month for the rest of my life.

I arranged to meet Tracy at the station. Standing by the barrier, I looked out for a flight-attendant-type woman. All I knew about Tracy was that she was blonde and American. I envisioned someone impossibly groomed and made-up; there would be, I was certain, frosted eye-shadow and acrylic nails. The blonde woman waving frantically as she walked towards me didn't seem to fit that description, though: in fact, I realised with alarm, it was even more worrying – she was wearing Winnie-the-Pooh dungarees! I, to use the American vernacular, don't 'do' Disney, and I have a special loathing for Walt's rape of an English literary classic. Tracy was beaming as she came towards me, arms outstretched for a hug, and my very British heart sank.

Of course, as it turned out, Tracy and I hit it off straight away and we remain friends to this day. Aside from her unfortunate Disney habit, it seemed that we had much more in common than I could have imagined. Like me, Tracy had been married twice and had one child, also a son, from that first relationship before having a daughter and identical twin boys with her second husband. Underneath the cutesy clothes and fluffy exterior, my new friend turned out to be a wise-cracking, chain-smoking girl after my own heart with a past almost as racy as my own and a nice line in self-deprecating humour. Indeed, sartorial issues aside, she could almost have been English.

That night, after visiting Felix and Theo, Tracy and I sat up talking. Her twins had been premature and had spent their first weeks in the hospital, so she understood the almost physical longing as I waited to get them home. It was good to share stories with someone who had been through something so similar. She'd also dealt with disability; one of her twins was diagnosed with Asperger's Syndrome (a mild form of autism) and she told me about another online group for parents of twins where one or both kids had special needs. It seemed that a consequence of the high rate of prematurity among multiple births was a correspondingly high level of disability, and though I wouldn't have wished such an outcome on anyone, I was glad to find that I was far from alone.

Tracy and I talked about how hard it was to stay positive sometimes, and I told her that 'visualisation' was one of my most successful strategies. For this I created in my head an imaginary picture of me with Felix and Theo, all at home together, some day in the future. In my mind's eye the boys are around four years old and they stand before me while I am telling them off for some minor crime. Felix, the more impish of the two, is looking at me solemnly: he is wearing a Batman cape and mask, slightly askance. Theo, my sweet daydreamer, on the other hand, is not listening to the scolding at all because he is too busy being entranced by his own shoes, which are sparkly. I built up this picture with great attention to detail, embellishing and refining it every day. A future memory for me to aim at and a happy, ordinary life for me to believe in.

* * *

It never rains but it pours. Seriously, as if all the drama and worry about the twins was not enough, it seemed that fate had not quite finished dumping on me. As Felix and Theo hit the three-month mark, I was called in for a smear test in order to follow up on the problems that had been identified during my pregnancy. The test showed that, no, I was not one of those women whose dodgy cells spontaneously correct themselves; I would need to have a biopsy to get rid of the problem. It was, they assured me, quick and painless, absolutely nothing to worry about.

I am not, by nature, one of life's big worriers. If someone tells me not to worry then, generally, I won't. I can't say I was exactly looking forward to having part of my cervix sliced off, who would be? But, with all my energy and anxiety focused on Felix and Theo (or 'Fee-o an Fee-o' as Evie had taken to calling them) I was pretty sanguine about my upcoming date with the gynaecologist.

I had the biopsy under general anaesthetic. I'd been offered the choice between general and local and picked the former: I may not be a worrier, but I am pretty squeamish; it was better for everyone that I was unconscious. I think I was also quite looking forward to a couple of hours of being comatose. The daily drama of the babies was certainly starting to take its toll, and the thought of mentally escaping from it all, however briefly, was definitely appealing.

Danny collected me from the clinic after the biopsy and took me home to bed so that I could sleep off the anaesthetic. The next day I was fine, if a little sore, and I resumed my maternal and hospital duties, glad to have got the whole thing over and done with. It would be a week until I actually got the full results from the lab, but the doctor had told Danny that everything looked good so I put it all out of my mind. I have known dozens of women go through this procedure with no problems; all I expected when I did get the results was to be formally discharged from treatment.

Of course, I should have realised by this point that nothing in my life was going to be straightforward. This may have been a simple procedure for countless women I knew, but for me everything was suddenly seeming much more complicated. The lab results showed that not all the problematic cells were removed with the biopsy. I think I actually gave out a weary sigh as the gynaecologist broke the news: it suddenly seemed horribly inevitable. She started to go through my options for the next stage of treatment. We could do another biopsy, she told me, sketching out the familiar diagram of a womb – a slightly rounded triangle with the fallopian tubes at the top and cervix at the bottom – and marking another slice of cervix for removal. This might be enough, she told me, but there was also a possibility that we would miss some cells again. The doctor held her pencil over the drawing, pausing briefly; she then drew three heavy red lines across it. 'Your other option is a hysterectomy,' she told me; and then adding, somewhat unnecessarily, 'where we remove the whole womb.'

Fuck. I *really* wasn't expecting that! I wasn't prepared, not at all. Now I cursed my non-worrying nature. Paranoia would have at least had me mentally rehearsing the worst-case-scenario outcome, but here I was, absolutely dumbfounded. I asked her what her medical opinion was, which course of action would she recommend? Definitely the hysterectomy. Absolutely, positively so. Better safe than sorry…already a mother of four children… not getting any younger, blah, blah, blah. I don't think I really heard very much of it. It wasn't exactly complicated, though: what was most important to me, my health or my fertility? I didn't *think* I wanted any more children, Danny and I had already decided that our family was complete. I was suddenly over-whelmed with tiredness: I just wanted this to be over. Amidst all the fear and worry about Felix and Theo, there was just no time or energy for dealing with my own health issues; I'd had enough. In a semi-daze I agreed to the surgery and was booked in for a few days later. It was only when I got outside that I started to shake. By the time I managed to phone Danny, I was crying.

In a final ironic twist of the knife, I started my period that evening. I hadn't had one since before getting pregnant with Evie. But now, with just days until I said goodbye to them forever, my body decided to give it one last hurrah. Oh joy.

Everything happened so quickly. I'd barely had time to orien-tate myself with this new situation before I was being wheeled into an operating theatre and doing that countdown thing. Ten, nine, eight, sev…

I think I was crying when I came round. There was pain, and half-light in the curtained room. Danny was there I think. Someone was cleaning dried blood from my stomach; new, beau-tifully cool and crisp sheets; an injection in my thigh. Sleep.

My next brush with consciousness was much more successful. I can't say I was entirely coherent but I was certainly manageably conversational. The nurse showed me the button attached to my wrist which would, when pressed, deliver a little burst of morphine into my bloodstream. And this time Danny was definitely there, sitting beside my bed looking anxious and drawn and probably wondering which member of his family was going to be hospitalised next.

The drugs ensured I spent the first twenty-four hours after the surgery in reasonably good spirits and very little pain. My ability to moderate drug taking had clearly not improved, though, and I was quite relieved when they took the morphine pump away. I'd taken a laptop into hospital with me so I could stay in touch with my Twins List friends throughout my stay. My first post-surgery letters were opiate-fuelled and rambling, but essentially cheerful. Then, as the euphoric and pain-killing effects wore off, I came down to earth with an enormous emotional and physical bang.

My whole body seemed to hurt. I had now been opened up and sewn back together along the same scar, three times in just over a year. This, combined with the bodily stress of carrying twins to term, put my physical resources at rock bottom: healing from this surgery was going to be slow and painful. Emotionally I was no better. The combination of post-operative depression, drug withdrawal and the monstrous strain of the past few months threw me into a black despair. I tried to write to my online community, but this time I was too consumed with sadness even to reach out for help. The reality of having lost my fertility hit me hard and, for the first time, I actually grieved for this cornerstone of my womanhood. Rationally, I knew the loss was minimal. It was highly unlikely that Danny and I would ever have wanted any more children and, with me pushing forty, time was running out anyway. Even if we did want more kids, the twins and their mystery illness would probably have put us off. We had no idea what they had, but the idea of perhaps inflicting it on another baby was unthinkable. But the menstrual cycle, in all its bloody, inconvenient and painful glory, was part of womanhood for me. The rhythm of my body, the ebbing and flowing of hormones and energy, was a constant backing track over which I laid my life, mood and creative energy. Now there was silence, nowhere to orientate myself. The enormity of what I had lost ripped through my heart. For the first time since Theo and Felix had been born, I allowed myself a tiny sliver of self-pity which rapidly spiralled out of control, and scared me with its intensity. It was a sharp lesson in the importance of staying positive. I simply could not afford to entertain such negative emotions, not yet.

As I slowly dragged myself back to equilibrium Danny and my mother organised a special treat for me. Medical permissions had been sought, little jackets and shoes had been bought, the twin buggy had been dusted off and, in a funny little role reversal, Felix and Theo came to visit me for a change. Their first proper outing and it was to another hospital! They didn't seem to mind, though, and they were both clearly excited by this sudden expansion of their horizons. For me, it brought a little respite from depression. I showed them off proudly to the nurses who were looking after me; it wasn't much, but it was *something*. I should have been showing them off to the whole world by now, getting irritated, like the other parents on the Twins List, by the endless questions and stupid comments of well-meaning but ignorant passers-by. Their babyhood was slipping away, everything I'd expected to go through: endless nappies, no sleep, chaos...

Where was it? I wanted it all; I wanted the life I'd been promised in all its haphazard, back-breaking glory. After they left, headed back to their own hospital and nurses, I crumbled again. I felt bereft, barren, robbed. Not only would I never again have my own newborn baby to hold, I wasn't even being allowed to savour the babyhoods of my little boys. It was unbearable, and no amount of positive thinking could stem the torrent of sadness that overwhelmed me.

I was discharged five days after my surgery with strict instructions to rest and to lift nothing heavier than a pint of milk for six weeks; I wouldn't even be able to cuddle my babies properly. I was so tired; everything felt difficult. Depression wrapped itself around me like a shroud; just continuing to put one foot in front of the other felt like the hardest thing in the world. If I'd been thinking rationally I'd have realised that much of my terrible mood was down to the physical demands and changes of the surgery but, of course, rational thought had been one of the first casualties of my hormonal swing. I had tried to hide the bleakness of my heart from Danny, with little success. I was just too sad to put on a convincing smile so, instead, I wept silently and miserably, a huddling mass of snot and tears, sitting beside him as he drove me home from the hospital.

At home Danny settled me on the sofa with a cup of coffee. I hated being so pathetic and, God knows, Danny had enough woe of his own without me upping the misery levels so dramatically. Great: now I could add guilt to the long list of crappy emotions rattling around my head. There was a parcel for me on the table, a gift, wrapped and ribboned. Despite my black mood, I smiled.

I defy anyone to not feel a little better when presented with a gift. Danny, my fantastic husband, must have got me a welcome-home treat; it's exactly the sort of thoughtful gesture that he's good at (and that makes me the envy of women everywhere). He came into the room as I was opening it, watching me with interest. It turned out not to be from him at all, and the contents could not have been more welcome or unexpected.

Inside the parcel was a large photograph album. The pages didn't have photos in, though; it was filled instead with letters. These were real letters, proper ink-and-stamp letters, not emails, from families on the Twins List. Tracy had organised the collection and put it together for me, and Danny had helped by deleting Tracy's email asking who wanted to get involved, from the Twins List when it arrived. Each letter offered words of encouragement and beautiful testaments of how much my family's story had touched their hearts. To have them physically like this, instead of the virtual letters I had been used to, felt incredibly personal and intimate. As I read I discovered something else. Each of these letters had been sent with money, a contribution towards a gift. Within a few days, I would be receiving a wooden rocking chair; bought by my virtual community for me to 'rock my babies to sleep in' once I got them home.

It was absolutely overwhelming, and so utterly unexpected. There was such love in this book of letters, genuine and affecting; for once in my life I was quite lost for words. The internet, so often seen as anti-social and isolating, a mechanism for weirdos and loners to find each other and share vileness, but this was something else. These people, scattered all around the world, had become my friends. And they had done what friends do: they had supported me through my darkest time, they had shown me love, compassion and understanding, and they had worked together to find a way to brighten my day. How could I resist? It would take a heart of solid rock to stay depressed in the face of such heart-warming tenderness. In my super-emotional state, by the time I'd finished reading the book of letters, I was actually crying tears of happiness rather than misery.

~ 11 ~

Normal is actually an incredibly elastic concept. Between the bouts of illness and the seemingly endless transferring from the regular children's ward at UCH (Galaxy) and the intensive care unit at Great Ormond Street and back, we actually did develop a routine with Felix and Theo. Spring had been and gone, and the summer sunshine had a way of making even the most dismal hospital space feel a little more welcoming. The boys had their own room at the side of the main ward and it was here that I spent most of the summer, getting to know my children. I tried to make it homely by bringing their own bright blankets, little bouncy-seats, toys and even music. I was besotted with them. Despite their obvious problems, I could see only how utterly perfect they were.

I know that, at the time, I found the life I was leading crushingly hard, with stress coiled around my guts and acrid nausea tainting every moment. And yet, in recall it doesn't seem so bad. My memories are sun-dappled, my boys are all smiles and softly powdered baby skin. That summer, though it was really filled with uncertainty and nameless fear, feels like an oasis, and in a way it was. What went before and what came after is, I suppose, what makes these months feel like the peaceful time. All my happy times, all the good memories I have of my beautiful twins are here. That summer feels far away; not through time, but through distance. I have come so far since then, my world has changed so much and everything looks different from where I am now. Looking back it's hard to get inside the person I was then, and memory has the quality of an old home movie, stuttering and scratchy looking, sun-bleached, soundless; a picture of another woman on another day.

The boys themselves got more delightful by the day and I would spend hours lying on the bed with them, watching them play with each other's hands or noses: they didn't really need toys at all. I loved buying clothes for them, choosing outfits and dress-ing them up being one of the few parental tasks still available to me and, despite swearing that I would never do it, I was unable to resist dressing them in matching outfits and sending their cuteness quotient through the roof. I bought little all-in-ones for them, a cowboy print on Felix's and tropical flowers on Theo's, after which we called him Hawaii-Five-Theo and amused ourselves by posing him in a surfer's stance. My mother and I would spend the lazy summer afternoons, a baby on each of our laps, making up silly songs for the boys and cracking jokes about 'whether Felix's bum looks big in that nappy'. The babies loved all the attention, and would giggle and wriggle with excitement, laughing along with us like they actually understood. Despite, or perhaps because of, the seriousness of the situation, we developed a nice line in flippant gallows-humour; only at my very lowest points did I lose the ability to laugh at myself and our situation. Indeed, there were times when laughter was really the only sane reaction.

The boys were rapidly becoming mini celebrities in both of the hospitals. Even allowing for maternal bias, it was clear that they really were incredibly charming, and their extraordinary love for each other attracted comment from everyone. Nurses from other wards would even drop by our room just to see the babies who never let go of each other's hand, even when they were asleep. Indeed, their attachment was such that they were allowed to be nursed in the same cot even during admissions to intensive care (a previously unheard-of occurrence).

Theo and Felix had been booked to go back to Great Ormond Street for their gastrostomy surgery and, with sickening inevitability, when the day finally rolled around they got ill. They had both just recovered from one infection that had put them back into intensive care and were now on a surgical ward awaiting the surgeon's go-ahead and, true to form, they were both going downhill again. They were just shy of eleven weeks old and weighed just ounces more than they had at birth. Theo's chest sounded terrible and he'd been put in an oxygen box (a Perspex box over his head with oxygen pumped into it) which was making him utterly miserable. It took a lot to shake his sunny and uncomplaining disposition; his unhappiness was a clear indication of how ill he really was. Felix was only slightly better and I could only keep him calm by holding him in my arms and pacing the ward. The surgeon came to see them with his team; they wanted Felix in theatre that afternoon. I was shocked: surely he was far too ill? I was terrified, he was so frail, so tiny. I really wasn't sure that he would survive the surgery. I held him tight, tears in my eyes, as the surgeon explained that, with his constant aspirations, he might not ever get well enough to do the surgery without risk. It was a classic dilemma: he needed to be well for the surgery but it was the surgery that offered the best chance of getting him well.

Now where was my maternal instinct? I searched my heart for an answer – what should I do? Nothing came: I had reached the limit of my own knowledge with no option but to trust the experts and put my baby's life in their hands. I cried as I signed the consent form, I don't think I had ever been so scared in my life. That afternoon I was allowed to go down to theatre with him. They let me stay until the moment he'd been put to sleep, and then I was instantly and unceremoniously ejected. In the tightly chore-ographed dance of an operating theatre, distressed mothers are super-surplus to requirements. Standing in the hospital corridor, clutching Felix's blanket, tears streaming down my face, I suddenly had an urge to laugh at the sheer, ludicrous *poignancy* of it all. My life had become a grimly mawkish made-for-TV movie and, despite the terrible ache in my heart, I really could, at that moment, see the comedy in it.

Whenever either of the babies was having a 'good day', I had taken to going for walks around the hospital with him in my arms, invariably ending up in the hospital chapel. Now, with my thoughts and emotions in disarray, I headed there again in the hope of some divine intervention. Great Ormond Street Hospital has an extraordinary little chapel; Oscar Wilde was a fan, calling it 'the finest private chapel in London', and it remains as impressive today. Originally sited on the first floor of the hospital, the whole chapel was moved during the hospital refurbishment, brick by brick, to its present location on the ground floor. As a room, it has huge delusions of grandeur: a tiny little church, no bigger than a regular sitting room, which thinks it's a cathedral. Every inch of this beautiful baroque chapel is richly decorated with stained glass, golden carvings, ornate flourishes, jewel-bright colours and sugary depictions of biblical children. It should all be far, far too much but for some reason, perhaps just architectural chutzpah, the chapel gets away with it. I loved to sit on one of the little pews with Felix or Theo in my arms, and enjoy a few moments of peace, rocking my baby and watching the sunlight dance across the stained glass. Of course, this being Great Ormond Street, the hospital's darker reality is never far from the surface. As you enter the chapel there is an intercessional book, a notebook where people can write their prayers and ask for blessings. But in a hospital for sick children it becomes a testament to parental desperation. Page after heart-breaking page, parents plead with God for operations to be successful, for diagnosis to be benign, for their child to live. It is emotion at its most raw from people at their most vulnerable, and it is impossible to remain unmoved by it. The thought of something happening to our children is such a primal fear: it connects directly with our most fundamental instincts and can trigger us to act in ways that would otherwise be unthinkable. Doctors and nurses working in paediatric intensive care are well aware that the parents of critically ill children can be irrational, aggressive and erratic, clutching the flimsiest of straws and holding on to the unlikeliest of hopes. The intercession book in Great Ormond Street Hospital paints a picture of parenthood that is bloody and painful and heavy with nauseous anxiety. And yet it is here, stripped of the feel-good factor of nativity plays and first teeth, that the incredible nature of a father's love or a mother's promise is most apparent; here, in these tear-stained pages of desperate love, I always see something of the real and terrible essence of parenthood.

The hospital has a full ministry, including an Anglican vicar, a Jewish chaplain and a Muslim imam. I have often wondered at how difficult a job they have. How do you explain, to anguished parents as they watch their child suffer, or receive a diagnosis that is heavy with bleakness? How do you defend your God and preach his love, when a child's innocence is rewarded with pain and fear, or worse? It must be hard to convince people of a loving, purposeful divinity amid so much evidence of random chaos.

When your child is in surgery at GOSH you are given a pager and told not to leave the immediate vicinity of the hospital. In the event of something going wrong or unexpected complications during the operation, parents need to be nearby in order to give consents or make on-the-spot decisions, sometimes of life-and-death significance. As you might imagine, this makes an already stressful time immeasurably tenser. Outside the hospital entrance stand mutely anxious parents in ones or twos, burning through cigarettes, cartoon-like, seemingly in a single drag. I'd been a non-smoker for some time but, nevertheless, after my visit to the chapel, I found myself pacing the street outside with the other grimly terrified parents.

The operation took a couple of hours and my expectation that time would drag was unfounded. In fact it seemed Felix was out in the blink of an eye. They took him straight to intensive care and I was called to the unit just as they were settling him in. He was still unconscious with a ventilator tube taped to his nose. There was a new scar running virtually the full length of his tummy; fresh and bloody with stitches and tape to hold it together. The new gastrostomy tube was sited just underneath his bottom rib. I took one look at him and it felt like my heart would break; seeing him like this was almost more than I could bear. My little one, my beautiful boy, sliced and drugged and so desperately ill. I could not have hurt more if it had been me lying there post-operative. A huge wave of guilt crashed over me; oh God, what if it *was* my fault? What if it really was something I had done or even thought that had caused the babies' illness? How could I live with myself? Guilt, fear and grief fought for supremacy; nothing had prepared me for seeing my child like that, and I didn't know how I was supposed to bear it.

By the time Theo had his surgery, a couple of days later, Felix was out of intensive care and on the mend. I was better prepared to see Theo after the operation: I knew what to expect and, though it still felt like a knife in the heart to see him suffer, this time it didn't rip me apart. Theo bounced through the surgery and the recovery period too. I was overjoyed; I'd actually come to expect things to go wrong, so to have it all happen so smoothly felt like a gift. For once my twins were doing things by the book and, by the end of the week, they were both well enough to go back to Galaxy ward from where they could be discharged home.

The surgery did make a difference to their overall health and this, combined with the fact that it was summer and generally less germy, gave us real reason to be optimistic about getting them home. It was complicated, though, even with the boys in relatively good health. Evie was still not walking and the twins needed constant supervision: their inability to swallow effectively meant that they needed frequent suctioning, in order to clear saliva and other secretions from the back of their throats and keep them from choking. With Danny at work it was clear that it would be impossible for me to be alone with the children during the day; it simply would not be safe. I didn't want to put Evie into nursery. I felt strongly that she was too young and, in any case, I had waited so long to get my family all together in one place that I couldn't bear the thought of her being somewhere else.

Our local health authority agreed that I would need help and proposed a package of support that included a daytime health care assistant from Monday to Friday as well as three nights of nursing cover each week. Two carers were appointed, a local nursing agency was instructed to find staff for the night shifts, and the hospital would be responsible for seeing everyone was trained in the boys' care. That included Danny and me, of course. I had been suctioning the twins for some time and was, by this point, quite a dab hand at clearing their little throats of secretions, but I also needed to know how to suction their tiny nasal passages. Then there was the gastrostomy care to learn, how to unblock the tube, or change it when unblocking failed. I learned, along with Danny, my mother and my brother Charlie, how to set up monitors and to recognise signs of respiratory distress. We were all sent for resuscitation training, a day of teaching us how to deal with respiratory or cardiac arrest. I knew that some of the mothers on the Twins List, especially those whose babies had been very premature, had been trained in resuscitation (or CPR as it's known in the States) as a condition of getting their babies home: now it was happening to me. Sitting in the hospital teaching room, desperately trying to breathe life into the plastic lungs of the dummy baby I'd been given, I prayed that I'd never have to use this new skill. I was having trouble remembering the teaching from an hour earlier: there was no way I was going to be able to remember these complex instructions weeks, or even months, from now.

We were allocated a social worker; I was starting to get an inkling of the number of people who were going to be involved with our family. We were, it seemed, going to have to sacrifice privacy as a small platoon of therapists and professionals trekked through our life, asking questions and making notes on everything from the amount of pee produced by Felix and Theo each day, to the state of my marriage. It was bizarre being the subject of so much scrutiny, and occasionally alarming, but it also felt purposeful and, most of the time, I was optimistic and positive about our ability to cope with all these new challenges.

I met another Twins List mother, Linda, and we hit it off immediately. A Jewish New Yorker married to an investigative journalist and with twins (a boy and a girl) just a little older than Evie, we found we had much in common, from our left-wing political leanings, politically active past and hippyish roots, to a certain sardonic humour and shared acknowledgement that, whilst we loved our children beyond measure, there was more to life than just motherhood. When Linda and her family all moved to London for a while I was delighted, and we developed a deep friendship that endures to this day. Linda was actually one of the people who kept me sane through all the trauma. I am, in general, not someone who has vast numbers of friends; I have very few casual relationships preferring, instead, to have a couple of close friendships with people to whom I feel really bonded. Linda was one of the few people who really did hold my hand through the worst times, and I am immensely grateful for that. It can't have been easy, befriending someone whose life was in such turmoil; certainly most people instinctively backed away from Danny and me, perhaps afraid of catching whatever freakishly bad luck was swirling around us. So my friendship with Linda gave me some much-needed respite from the drama of my daily life and, more importantly, helped me see myself as something other than the mother of two very sick little boys.

In between the planning meetings, training sessions and nerve-wracking bouts of illness from the boys, I was actually getting quite adventurous with Felix and Theo. With a suction machine hanging off the back of the buggy we'd even managed a couple of short walks around the West End. On these momentous occasions, I would have the boys scrubbed and polished and dressed in their cutest outfits. I was beyond proud, positively shimmering with love for them and a desire to show them to the world. And the world, it has to be said, seemed impressed because we would be showered with compliments and approval and, by the time we got back to the ward, I would be almost tearful with joy. We even managed a couple of visits to the magical kingdom of 'home' where, just for a few hours, we could imagine that we were a normal family leading an average life. I was learning to grab my happiness where I could, and to be grateful for it.

The boys' discharge always seemed to be just out of reach. Danny and I would joke about the hospital's 'mythical two weeks' as this was always the answer to the question 'when are we likely to be able to take them home?' The truth was, of course, that no one knew when they'd be strong enough, so 'two weeks' became shorthand for 'I don't really know because we don't know what's actually wrong with them, but not today, or tomorrow, or even this week, but soonish. Probably.'

It was hard. Despite the sun-drenched days and the absolute delightfulness of Theo and Felix, and despite the super-human effort I put into staying positive, sadness sat like a lump in my throat, never forgotten and never far from the surface. I cried a lot, from fear and sorrow and exhaustion, but there was never any choice but to cope.

There were also blessings though, and even in the worst times I could see them. My love for Danny grew stronger every day. Whatever was happening to our life, to our family, we were in it together; and I could not imagine another soul that I could have shared this journey with. My husband and I are very different people and we deal with crises in very different ways. I reach out: I write and talk and spill my guts across the bloody page. Danny is more private in his pain, he rarely cries or opens up his heart. And yet we could not have been more united. Synchronised at every step we found a harmony; it was so easy to walk together and I was filled with love for my husband and immense gratitude that I didn't have to make this journey alone.

Officially the position with Danny's family remained the same, but the extremeness of our situation had some unexpected effects, and we were just beginning to see signs of a softening in attitude. Most of Danny's close relatives (grandparents, aunts, uncles and cousins) knew about his marriage and children by this point although very few had actually met me. My mother-in-law was a regular visitor to both the hospital and our house and all of Danny's surviving grandparents had been to meet their great-grandchildren. Danny's mother, Anne, was even keeping her husband up to date with the babies' progress and I can only imagine how hard it must have been for him to be disconnected from us at such a worrying time, torn between religious duty and parental concern. One night, when Danny called to update his mother, his father answered the phone and, rather than passing the call to his wife as expected, he asked after the boys himself. It seems a tiny thing, but Danny knew how much it meant. His children, his family, were being acknowledged in his father's house. We never expected it, never believed it would happen, but it had. People have asked me why I wasn't angry about the situation with Danny's father; some have even expressed incredulity, assuming (wrongly) that I *was* angry and was either hiding it or in denial. Perhaps it was because there was absolutely nothing personal in the estrangement, and that had been made quite clear to me from the very start. Maybe it was because I was aware that, for Danny's father, this was a huge personal sacrifice. Absolutely everything I had heard about the man told me that giving up his relationship with his grandchildren would be devastating for him, a heart-breaking loss for a man who, as a leader of his community, felt he had no option but to, quite literally, practise what he preached. Whatever the reasons, the fact is that I truly didn't feel angry, just sad for my husband and for my father-in-law, and hopeful that we would find a way to be reconciled one day.

I continued to update the Twins List most days. Having met Tracy and Linda now I felt even more bonded to the group. Like Felix and Theo, I had good and bad days. My hysterectomy had knocked me hard emotionally, the recovery was much tougher than I'd expected and I credited my daily outpourings, and the huge swell of support and sympathy, with keeping me from going under completely.

> 'Felix and Theo are five months old today. Wow! Almost half of their first year gone already and still we wait to get them home. I dread these days, I always feel so robbed on the anniversaries. Their babyhood is slipping away from us and we will never get it back. It's hard to be strong at these times – I still ache for them all the time, we all do, and long for my family to be together. Each month I say "well it won't be too long now" and this time maybe that's true – Please God.'

The boys were recovering from another virus, and were more or less back to their normal selves. Theo though, was still requiring oxygen and it was looking increasingly likely that he would be coming home on it because of his chronic lung problems. His lungs, the doctors assured me, would eventually improve as he got bigger and grew new, unscarred, tissue but, for the time being, he was going to need the extra help.

I was bringing Evie up to the hospital a couple of times a week, and she was absolutely delighted by her baby brothers, wanting to cuddle and stroke them constantly. Felix actually seemed a little scared of her and her exuberant toddler-love, but Theo was fascinated by his big sister and would gaze at her, as though awestruck, for hours. I treasured these times with my little ones and, even in the bustling hospital environment, we managed to snatch little crumbs of 'normal' family life. The boys grew lovelier by the day. Theo was so dreamy most of the time, happy to just stroke something that felt nice or listen to his favourite song; Felix, though, was a terrible flirt with (even at just five months) an eye for a pretty nurse. Both boys, in very different ways, were real little characters, and I knew they would be deeply missed on the ward when they finally did go home. They loved visitors, lighting up whenever anyone came into their room, and I was certain that they were really going to adore being part of our family.

We discovered the babies had a problem with their autonomic systems (which governs things like heart rate and body temperature). They were constantly soaked with sweat even though I changed their clothes several times a day. At first the doctors assumed that this was a side-effect of the drugs they were being given but, eventually, drugs were ruled out and it was deemed 'part of their (still unknown) condition'. The doctor who broke the news to me was essentially reassuring, telling me that there shouldn't be any long-term implications of their increased heart/respiratory rate. A few days later, their consultant told me that 'in the long list of their difficulties, this is really the least of their problems' and, I swear, I didn't know whether to laugh or cry.

Despite my regular bouts of sadness, though, I never stopped giving thanks for my angel babies. I could no longer imagine our life without them; even at my lowest points (and there were many) I could always see the joy they had brought and the profound lessons we had been taught, and I never lost hope for our future together. I knew that what really counted in any family was happiness and love, and I knew that no disability could prevent us from having that.

My internet friends continued to do whatever they could to cheer and encourage me. On Tracy's next visit to our house she presented me with a gift bag that had, written on the front, the words 'here's the proof that dreams really do come true'. Inside, remembering the story I had told her of my imaginary picture of my children at home, she had made a tiny Batman cape for Felix and a pair of minute sparkly shoes for Theo. The babies looked gorgeously comical in their little outfits and I was moved again by the extraordinary kindness I was being shown.

I was also given an opportunity to stand on the other side of the Twins List experience. Although there are (or were) around fifteen hundred families subscribed to the group, the number who regularly contribute to the daily chatter is much smaller. Most subscribers are 'lurkers', invisible readers who rarely physically post unless they have a specific question. As well as the lurkers, every internet community I have been involved with has a small (relative to the number of subscribers) group of members who post regularly, respond to any questions they can, post useful information and links to other sites and swap tips and tell jokes. These are the people who give the group its character and sense of community. Most members will go through phases of being more or less involved and each community sets its own parameters of acceptable posting material and length. What this means is that, even with fairly large communities, you can still get to know people well because the group feels much smaller. One of the most active members when Felix and Theo were born was an expectant American mother called Shannon. Already a mother of one child, Shannon joined the group early in her twin pregnancy, around the time my boys were born. She was from Seattle, a sassy, smart and funny girl, quite young and glamorous but financially precarious and in an uncertain relationship with the twins' father. Life was certainly no easy ride for her, but no one doubted her ability to hold it all together; she was one of those tough women with a big heart who gets on with the life she's been dealt without complaints or self-pity. Shannon, despite her rocky private life, was delighted and excited to be expecting twins and soon became an active and well-liked member of the group and someone with whom I'd been swapping banter for months.

Twenty-two weeks into her pregnancy, just shy of the lower limit for foetal viability, an unnoticed cervical infection caused Shannon to lose first one and then, within a few hours, the other baby. Two little boys, Nicholas and Matthew: I still remember their names even after all this time. Shannon's email, containing such heartbreaking news, dropped into my inbox like any other post. The subject line read 'Sad news – get a tissue' and I sat at my computer and wept for the loss of a woman halfway across the world who I'd never met, and likely never would. Shannon and I had such different lives; there was so little common ground. Our ages, backgrounds, interests, politics: in almost every way we were different and, under normal circumstances, it was impossible to imagine a situation that would cause our paths to cross. And yet in cyberspace we were friends, neighbours even; there was a connection that was real and meaningful. I mourned Shannon's loss as I would have mourned for any friend going through something so terrible, and I desperately wanted to help. We all did. Grief and shock rippled around the Twins List and normal chatter gave way to condolences and concern and expressions of sadness and disbelief. Someone who lived near to Shannon got details of the funeral for us and many people sent flowers. Poor Shannon was, of course, heartbroken, but I know it brought some comfort for her that so many people wanted to remember her boys and her loss.

The outpouring of love from the group over the next few days was extraordinary. It quickly became clear that many people wanted to do something more practical to help Shannon and her family through such a terrible time. With money so tight, Shannon was worried about not being able to get a proper tombstone for their tiny grave and a collection was quickly organised. In the end, there was more than enough money raised and, just as had happened with my rocking chair, after the intended purchase a donation was made to an appropriate charity. (In my case, this was to a charity that supports families while their children are in hospital. Money left over after Shannon's stone was paid for went to research into miscarriage.)

I was immensely moved by the compassion and overwhelming desire to help that was shown by the list. Even though I had been

on the receiving end of such generosity of spirit, it was being part
of the wave of love for Shannon that really opened my eyes to the
fact that there was nothing 'virtual' about this community; it was
as real and concrete as any village. And it was one that I was
incredibly proud to belong to.

~ 12 ~

There are times when life happens so fast that events tumble over each other, great rolling waves of confusion that wash over a fractured world. Sometimes all you can do is run, racing cartoon-like against the burning fuse. You never know what's just around the corner. Actually, at times, you don't even know what's right under your feet.

Incredibly, and in spite of the boys' gut-wrenching, three-steps-forward-two-steps-back progress, we were finally getting realistically near to a discharge. Our health authority had engaged two carers to help me during the days, my family and I had all been trained, a huge amount of equipment and supplies had been delivered to our home and Theo and Felix seemed to be in reasonable health. The house, already too small for our family, was now positively bulging at the seams with all the extra kit we needed. Theo, as predicted, was coming home oxygen-dependent so we'd been given an oxygen compressor. We'd also been sent an oxygen engineer who had drilled holes through the living room ceiling in order to run oxygen tubing upstairs, so that Theo could be bathed each night. The babies would sleep in our bedroom when we were without help and, on the nights when we had a nurse working, they'd sleep in the travel cot in the living room. It was far from ideal but at least we'd all be under the same roof and, by this point, I was ready to suffer any inconvenience or discomfort to make that happen. The night before discharge, I wrote to the list.

'How do I feel? Tired... It's been such a long journey to get here. I'm also very proud of all of us as a family and the way we have pulled together and come through. I'm a little nervous about the future, of course; but I have faith that we will continue to stick together as we meet our challenges and, in the end, that's what really counts. I am grateful for everything too. It's true; I believe that our lives are richer, our family is stronger and, despite everything, we are actually happier. I count my blessings every day, I never did that before but I have learned to appreciate everything I have and that's such a gift. My children are beautiful, all four of them and, for the first time in my life, I've actually learned to believe that I really am a good mother and that I can trust myself and my instincts for them. And what do we mean by healthy anyway? A healthy and happy heart is what's important and no physical challenges need damage that. I still know that God **never** makes mistakes and that my boys are perfect in every way.

I would never have chosen this path, I would never have had the imagination; but I am honoured to have been allowed to walk it anyway. We've met incredible people, been shown love beyond belief by complete strangers and had our faith strengthened on a daily basis – who could ask for more?'

I didn't imagine there would be too many more of the updates. I wrote my letter to the list almost as an epitaph, believing that, from that point onwards, we would just be getting on with our lives as another normal family, with all the chaos that four kids, three of whom were under eighteen months, entailed. I thanked my list-mates for giving me space to sound off for five and a half months; I genuinely didn't know what I would have done without it. Since the babies' dramatic entrance all those months earlier, I'd had doctors and social workers regularly asking me if I had enough emotional support; it was hard to explain just how incredibly strong this invisible safety net below me was.

I hardly dared allow myself to breathe, let alone hope. There had been so many disappointments and so many false dawns, I was almost paralysed with prayer that all would go smoothly. Day by day the complex arrangements fell into place and eventually I started to let myself believe that it was really happening. Danny and I were both incredibly excited: we'd waited so long for this and the journey had been so very hard. On the day itself, Danny made a beautiful photograph of the twins into a goodbye picture for the nurses, and I bought a frame for it, as well as the biggest cake I could find. Felix and Theo would have a proper send-off on the ward; after months of uncertainty and drama, getting them home felt like an achievement for everyone.

Did you think it was all going to go right? Of course not! At the very last minute we hit a snag. I had held back from believing it would be OK for as long as humanly possible; I couldn't bear to be disappointed again but, finally, I peeped over the parapet and *BANG!* Right between the eyes.

I arrived at the hospital on the day we were supposed to be taking them home, to find that Theo was brewing a cold. It wasn't anything terrible or desperately serious, just a cold, but he was definitely under the weather. I felt like I'd been punched, emotions I didn't even have names for. This last-minute disappointment, after everything we'd already been through, was just too awful. I was speechless with anguish and, looking at the faces of the doctors and nurses around me, I could see that they were gutted too. The consultant came to see Theo. Yes, she agreed, he did seem to be a little unwell but it was very minor. Her real concern was that winter was now approaching: if we didn't get the boys out of hospital soon they were going to get caught up in the snot season. Hospitals are pretty germy places at the best of times, but in the winter months they are breeding grounds for viruses and bacteria, exactly the sort of place you would want to avoid if you were a baby with serious respiratory issues. Despite Theo being at less than top form, this might be our best chance to get the babies home: if we missed the window, they might be stuck in hospital until spring.

The consultant felt we should still take them home. Not only was the hospital going to be an increasingly hazardous place for the next few months, but Danny and I were more than prepared. We had been trained, we knew our babies extremely well and, most importantly, we would have a qualified nurse on duty at home that night; we would not be alone. In addition to all this, Theo was really not very sick at all. In any other child his slight sniffle would have barely warranted comment. It was agreed: our boys were coming home.

I could have kissed her. I was ecstatic with relief and now, with everything cleared, I could really give vent to my joy. My babies were coming home! We didn't even stay to share the cake I'd bought for the nurses; one quick round of thanks and hugs and we were gone.

I wanted to enjoy every moment of this day. Even strapping the babies' two little seats into the car, something which would undoubtedly become a chore very soon, was an event to be savoured. And we were so ready for this homecoming, physically and emotionally: I'd played the whole fantasy through in my head so many times it almost felt like déjà vu. It seemed as though we had been through a war and walking through the front door, me holding Felix and Danny with Theo, felt like our own incredible victory parade. I sat in the living room, surveying the happy domestic scene about me. Evie, who was still not walking (she was actually a very late walker), was shuffling on her bottom from one baby to the other and back again, with increasing confidence, scavenging whatever dummies, toys, socks or blankets she could prise off them. Theo couldn't take his eyes off her; clearly he was besotted with his big sister. Felix, on the other hand, was most entranced by the television, staring at it with goggle-eyed awe.

Even Joey, who as a typical adolescent spent most of his time ferreted away up in his bedroom, had deigned to join us downstairs. The room felt cosy and cheerful; Danny and I were absolutely glowing with satisfaction and pride.

> 'This is just a quick note to let you know that Felix and Theo are now officially resident at **HOME!** Yes, we finally made it after 172 days in hospital – our sweet babies are **home home home**. Theo is a little unwell, he spiked a fever briefly last night and he is a bit snotty but **HE'S HOME!** We felt that if we carried on waiting for a day when everything was 'perfect' then we would probably never get them home at all.'

Once the novelty of this new source of entertainment and 'stuff' wore off, Evie was, unsurprisingly, rather overwhelmed by the arrival of her brothers. I made a mental note that she would need lots of extra love and reassurance over the following week or so. Mummy time, I realised, might be a little difficult to find but we'd manage somehow; at least we were, *finally*, all in the same place.

Later that afternoon, a couple of the community nurses dropped by to see how we were doing. They found us happy, settled and calm. I think they were quite taken aback by how well-prepared and on top of the situation we were but, given that we'd had months to get ready for this, perhaps it shouldn't have been that surprising to find everything running so smoothly. The boys sat in their little chairs, wriggly and excited, and smiled and gurgled for our visitors, clearly enjoying both the non-institutional setting and all the attention they were getting. Danny and I were beaming, relishing every second of this much longed-for event. Evie and Joey were just glad to have their parents back: it was easy to forget that these months had been hard on them too. For the first time in a long time, I actually started to relax.

That evening, before the night nurse arrived, I got everything ready for the babies' first bedtime at home. Danny and I bathed them and laid them, pink and damp and smiley, on our bed to be powdered and pyjama-ed. Back downstairs I settled them in their cot and connected them to their monitors. The readings for both babies were fine; Theo's heart rate and oxygen levels were actually much better than they had been in the hospital, and I put his improvement down to his being at home. Both boys were getting fed continuously overnight and I connected each of their tummy tubes to their little feeding pumps, primed them with milk and set the rate to a steady drip that would see them get all of their calories by the morning. Then I labelled them. Danny laughed at me as I stuck little name tags on each piece of equipment, each wire and, finally, each baby. To me they looked very different and I had no problem telling them apart, but they were identical twins and their differences were far too slight to be spotted by the casual observer. I can, when need arises, be incredibly organised and methodical and by the time the nurse arrived, I had laid out everything she might need including written notes on their care, and coffee and biscuits to fortify her through the small hours. Finally, after triple-checking everything,

I did what I had been waiting almost six months to do: I kissed all of my sleeping children before crawling, tired and happy, into my own bed.

The tap on the door came around six in the morning. I was awake instantly and out of bed like a bullet. Danny has often remarked on my astonishing ability to be fully conscious in milliseconds when – and *only* when – one of my children is in trouble.

I flew down the stairs and into the living room. It's extraordinary how fast a mother's brain can work in a crisis. One look at the cot and I knew immediately what was happening. Theo had stopped breathing: he lay blue-grey and motionless on his back; Felix was sleeping beside him. The babies were still connected to their pumps and monitors, and while Felix's monitor showed his oxygen levels at a healthy ninety-seven, Theo's was reading twenty. *Twenty?*! Shit, shit, *shit*! I screamed for Danny, grabbed Theo from the cot and laid my son on the floor. Just as I'd been trained, I began resuscitation. *Blow, pump, pump, pump, pump, pump; blow, one, two, three, four, five; blow...* Danny called for an ambulance; the nurse stood in mute shock and I asked her to take over the CPR for a moment. She tried but I could see immediately that she was too freaked out; I was doing a better job myself. I pushed her out of the way. *Blow, one, two, three, four, five; blow, one, two, three, four, five...* Where the fuck was the ambulance? Danny was waiting in the street for them while I worked on Theo; my mind was crystal clear, I had never been so focused in my life.

The ambulance crew didn't waste any time once they did eventually arrive. Arriving at the house, running up the stairs, grabbing Theo and leaving for University College Hospital, all in a matter of seconds. By the time they arrived, Theo's oxygen level was zero. Danny and I were wearing just dressing gowns; we would throw on some clothes and follow in the car with Felix. The nurse would have to stay behind with Evie and Joey until I could get a member of my family round there; there was no other choice and no time to discuss it. I prayed aloud all the way to the hospital: *'Please don't take my baby, please don't take my baby'*; but in my heart I didn't expect to find him alive when we arrived at the hospital.

I will never forget the scene in the resuscitation room that morning. Theo arrived at the hospital just as the day and night shifts were changing over, so there were twice as many doctors around as usual. Paediatricians came from Galaxy, the children's ward, as well as from the NICU where the babies had spent their first weeks. Theo lay unconscious on a table; there were so many people working on him that, at times, I couldn't see him at all. They couldn't find a decent vein in his hands or feet; months of drips and injections had made them all too frail: a nurse was shaving a patch of his hair so that they could get a line into his head. He'd been intubated and they were bagging breaths into his unresponsive little body. Someone was asking me how long he'd been without oxygen. No, no, *no*! I couldn't bear it; don't take his mind, his sweet little nature: it was all he had! The tears didn't stop streaming as I raged and pleaded silently with God and the universe, fate, luck, anything and everything to *give me my baby back*!

Incredibly they managed to get Theo stable enough to be

transferred to Great Ormond Street and he was whisked off to the PICU in an ambulance. I took Felix up to Galaxy ward; he needed to be checked over to make sure that he wasn't going to be following his brother. The ashen faces of the nurses up there told me that I was not the only one devastated by Theo's collapse. I was numb with misery and anguish. What were we to do now? I felt lost, utterly disconnected from normal life. It was decided that, as a precaution, Felix should be readmitted despite his apparent good health, and I handed him over mutely. I think Danny had gone home to relieve the nurse and sort out Joey and Evie; or maybe he had gone in the ambulance with Theo. In truth, I don't really remember. That morning remains in my memory as a hazy, dream-like blur, shot through with splinters of pin-sharp clarity.

Some time later that morning (an hour? two?) I found myself at Great Ormond Street with Danny, watching Theo's chest rise and fall and listening to the soothing, rhythmic sigh of the ventilator. He was still unconscious and we had no way of knowing how much damage, if any, had been done to his little brain. Once he was awake we would have a better idea, but it could be a long time until we really knew if he was going to be OK. Afterwards, as we walked through the streets, we talked about how strange it felt to see people going about their ordinary day. The events of our morning had been so huge, so earth-shaking, it seemed inconceivable that no one else had felt the tremor.

I told Danny he should speak to his father. There was a very real chance that Theo would not make it through this latest crisis and I felt that his grandfather should at least be given the opportunity to meet him. If we lost Theo now there could be no going back, no second chance. It seemed to me that if we missed this chance to reach out, we would all regret it forever.

So Danny called and asked his father to come and, of course, he came. In the midst of all the terrible fear and pain, a little spark of something beautiful. A tiny glimmer of good can light the darkest day, a scrap of hope to soothe our broken hearts.

~ 13 ~

Danny's parents lived a couple of hours away, but they came straight to the hospital. Theo was, of course, still unconscious and we were waiting anxiously to see whether he had suffered brain damage through being oxygen-deprived. It must have been quite a shock to my father-in-law, seeing his grandchild for the first time in such a terribly frail condition. After spending some time on the intensive care unit with Theo, we all adjourned to the hospital café where we could talk more easily.

This was the first time I had seen Danny with his father and I was struck by the obviously tender feelings between the rabbi and his son. It was a long way from the overpowering and authoritarian figure I had imagined; yet, of course, it made sense. Danny himself was a wonderful father to our children: he must have learned it somewhere. Over coffee we explained, as best we could, what was wrong with the babies and what had happened to Theo that morning. For the first time, Danny's father was able to ask questions and to show his concern for his son and his son's family. He wanted to know everything, not just about our children but about us, Danny and me: how were we coping with this ordeal? As Danny tried to give a brief outline of everything that we'd been through over the previous six months, I exchanged smiles with his mother. Despite the ordeal and distress of our current circumstances, there was an undeniable relief that we had bridged a seemingly unbridgeable gulf.

I listened to my husband as he recounted our recent journey; it never failed to surprise me how difficult and dramatic it sounded. And even though I knew that it really *was* difficult and dramatic, I'll admit there was still a sliver of my old way of thinking that told me I was making a fuss.

Looking back on that day, on that first meeting with Danny's father, I was bizarrely serene. I have noticed this phenomenon in myself and in other people from time to time, a strange human safety mechanism that protects us though life's darkest days. Extreme crisis sometimes produces a supernatural kind of calm as if our spiritual essence takes over, and lifts us high above the earthly pain. A few years ago, a friend of mine had breast cancer. Her mastectomy took place just days after she gave birth to her second child and, through it all, she exuded peacefulness and a quiet, graceful courage, that seemed to stem the natural rush to fear and grief whenever things got especially hard. Sometimes life is just so very sad that we simply cannot allow ourselves to fully feel it. I once heard someone in AA describing the 'rock bottom' that catapulted them into recovery in the words 'I was so low; I was in a state of grace'. I don't think I have ever heard it described better. So once Theo had been stabilised and was out of immediate danger, I think I must have found a way to rise above my feelings. Whatever the process, I was able to remain positive and serene through that first conversation, enough to impress my father-in-law. 'I can see why my son married you,' he told me as we said goodbye, and I knew that something fundamental had shifted.

Later that very same day Theo briefly regained consciousness. I was sitting by his bed, stroking his little hand and singing his favourite songs when he opened his eyes and smiled at me. That smile told me everything I needed to know. My darling Theo was still there, his brain undamaged: he could get better, we hadn't lost him. I cried ecstatic tears as I broke the news to Danny by phone. Astonishingly, Theo was going to be all right. How close had we come to losing him? Closer than close. I *know* that when I pulled him still and grey from his cot that morning I had, indeed, breathed life back into him. He had gone: just for a moment, but he had really gone; I had used a mother's burning love to drag him back to me.

I saved him. The ambulance men told us that only my quick thinking and well-recalled training had saved our son. When we were taught CPR I never thought that I would remember it, but I had underestimated the things a mother can do when her child is in danger. I saved him then. I saved his life, or so it seemed to everyone; but I knew he was not saved, merely stopped because I would not let him go.

'*I just don't know how to write this. All day we have waited to find out whether he would live. At one point all they would tell us was "he's alive for now". Finally we have been told – he is going to live and his EEG has shown that he has suffered no long-term brain damage despite being without oxygen for some time this morning. I thought we had hit bottom before in terms of fear and grief, we had not. I don't have words; I don't know where to start. My heart is breaking now. I have never seen Danny break down and sob before but this morning, when we thought our little Theo was gone, our whole world fell apart. He is not as quick or as much of a charmer as his twin, but baby Theo has the sweetest spirit and the gentlest nature that I have ever known in a child.'*

Theo was going to be in hospital for a long time, that much was clear; his lung had completely collapsed and it was going to take time to repair. I was, of course, grateful that his life had been saved, and that his brain hadn't been damaged through lack of oxygen, but I was incredibly sad for him, and for all of us. He was back to being fully ventilated, on a morphine drip and all alone. We were devastated. How many times would we have to watch our dream being snatched away? The previous night I had sat up planning our week: the places we were going to go, games to play together, things to do with Evie and Joey. I had been so happy – *so happy!* I hadn't even got twenty-four hours with them, and now my boys were both in different hospitals, with Theo critically ill and on life support. I didn't know how much more of this I could take; I had never felt so powerless and the nightmare seemed to just go on and on.

A few days later, on my way from home to the hospital, I was suddenly seized with terror. Something awful was going to happen, I felt sure. Perhaps I would be run over crossing the road or, please God, no – something was going to happen to Danny! I couldn't seem to stop crying, and I was filled with a fear of unnamed and unknown events. The realisation suddenly hit me: I no longer lived in a world where bad things happened to other people, they happened to me, and I was utterly convinced that they would not stop. Life was going to hurt me in unimaginable ways. I feared desperately for the people I loved.

After several days of almost constant tears, Danny gently suggested I see our GP. The doctor diagnosed depression (no shit!) and prescribed mild anti-depressants; I was grateful for anything that would help me regain a semblance of equilibrium.

Felix turned out to be fine; whatever bug Theo had got seemed to have bypassed him and so he was discharged from hospital almost immediately. He loved being home nearly as much as we loved having him at home. Despite being almost six months old, he was still a tiny little thing and Evie was enchanted with this smiley, wriggly 'dolly' we'd brought in. Theo actually bounced back from the worst of his close encounter with the Grim Reaper quite quickly, and was soon out of intensive care and transferred back to Galaxy. From there we would start the long haul back to discharge again; providing, of course, he didn't catch anything else.

Once again I found that even the most extraordinary circumstances can become routine. Each day I would bundle Felix up in his little coat, pack up milk, feeding tubes, suction catheters, nappies and the other million-and-one things that any mother carries, load the suction machine and Felix on to the buggy and set off for the hospital. Usually I'd have to stop halfway to suction Felix, my first experience of the kind of attention that people with disabilities get from strangers. These days I am an expert suctioner, performing the entire operation smoothly and almost without breaking stride. But, in those early months, I was anxious and inept, breaking into a nervous sweat and fumbling with catheters and gloves while Felix would be quietly changing colour by the side of the road, and passers-by would be looking at me with a mixture of horror and pity. We'd eventually get to the hospital where we would spend much of the day with Theo, and then head home to do the bath/story/bed routine with Evie. For almost three weeks we had something that bore a passing resemblance to a family life.

At home, Felix was making phenomenal progress. Because he was managing his saliva so much better, and needing far less suctioning, the speech therapist agreed that we could start trying to introduce oral feeding again. Milk was still considered too dangerous (the risk of aspiration being particularly high with liquids) so it was a *tiny* dab of apple puree, which Felix licked off the end of my finger that constituted his first solid 'meal'. He was still getting all the calories he needed from his overnight tube feeding; the apple was really just to introduce the concept of taste. As he poked suspiciously at the blob of goo on my fingertip, I realised the poor little thing was probably expecting trauma, not pleasure. I needed to show him that nice things could happen in his mouth as all he had ever known up until that point were tubes and suction catheters; no wonder he was looking so doubtful about the whole exercise. The puree was a success in that he didn't choke or (as far as I could tell) aspirate, but he didn't seem that impressed by this new experience either. Over the next few days I introduced him to a variety of tastes, including what I thought was a sure-fire winner: chocolate. Nothing really seemed to pique his interest, although he had a *slight* preference for salty over sweet flavours. What I didn't realise then was that Felix had very little sense of taste. His condition meant that, even before his tracheostomy, he didn't really breathe through his nose, just through his mouth. Without the all-important smell, there is little taste (ask anyone with a badly blocked-up nose). So my Felix, who, in any case, was being fed regularly by tube and therefore didn't get hungry like most kids, could barely taste the pureed carrots and mild baby foods I was offering him. No wonder he seemed nonplussed by the whole 'food thing'. Today Felix still doesn't eat as such; he gets all his nutrition from a special liquid diet that he receives via his gastrostomy. But, of course, nourishment is only one of the benefits of eating. It is also a social activity and a sensory pleasure and these are aspects that Felix can enjoy. As a bright and lively six-year-old, he loves to be part of mealtimes and, unsurprisingly, he wants to do the same things as his classmates and siblings. He has become extremely skilled at *pretending* to eat, and will happily sit at the table during family mealtimes pushing one pea and half a chip around his Spiderman plate, miming chewing and making appreciative yum-yum noises. He 'drinks' from a cup with a teaspoonful of water in it, and manages to make it look like the finest champagne. And he has even learned to appreciate taste, though it must be a very strong flavour indeed to fight its way through his inefficient olfactory system. Felix loves soy sauce and the teeniest spot on the end of his tongue sends him into a funny, frenzied little dance of excitement, his face lighting up with happiness over both the taste of the sauce, and his own daring in taking it.

Having to teach my child not to be afraid of food, that his mouth could be a source of pleasure not just pain, was just one of the ways that raising the twins was different from my other kids. There were so many of these hurdles, a million unexpected bumps in the road, consequences of their unorthodox start. But despite me discovering new implications of their extended hospitalisation every day, it was still wonderful to see Felix getting better and better. His strength was rapidly increasing and, at long last, his cry had even become loud enough that we could hear it from another room. I had high hopes that he would eventually overcome many of his disabilities.

Of course, watching the widening gap between the boys was a mixed bag of emotions for me. On the one hand, I was overjoyed for Felix who was doing just brilliantly but a big part of me just felt sadder and sadder for my darling Theo. As if the unfairness of the boys' circumstances wasn't difficult enough, having Felix home (and organising all his appointments and sessions) was making it doubly hard for me to see as much of Theo as I would have liked, at the exact time that I felt he needed me the most. It was hard to stay positive, but I forced myself to remain upbeat, telling Theo (and myself) that someone must be preparing him for an awfully big adventure through life, to have given him this extraordinary start. I prayed that once Theo did finally come home, he would catch up with his twin but, following his respiratory arrest, we were not being given any guarantees at all about that.

I also worried for Theo because Evie and Felix were really bonding at home, and I was afraid that Theo would be left out. Evie, after a suspicious start, now adored Felix, kissing him constantly and letting him stroke her face and hair as she lay beside him. It was unbelievably sweet to watch them, and she was incredibly gentle with her little brother, seeming to know instinctively how fragile he was. It was wonderful to see their blossoming friendship; I could happily watch them together for hours and feel completely at peace, all but for the little voice inside me that kept whispering 'this shouldn't be happening without Theo'.

Danny and I celebrated our first wedding anniversary with only Theo missing from home. That night, after the children had gone to bed, we sat and marvelled at the extraordinary direction our life had taken. It felt like we'd been married for so much longer than a year; we were barely recognisable as that couple with the perfect life we had seemed to be on our wedding day. Everything was different now and all traces of smugness had long since vanished, but I still knew that there was not another living soul I would rather have had by my side than my husband.

Theo improved each day; it really wouldn't be long before he was home. Unfortunately, and somehow inevitably, Felix came down with a bug just before Theo was ready for discharge. And so, rather like one of those barometer clocks where either the sunshiny lady or the rainy-day man pops out of the house, the boys swapped places and Felix went into hospital while Theo came home. It was so strange, dressing Theo in the little coat that Felix had worn. It was a hand-me-down duffle-coat that had originally been Evie's and so far, I noted ruefully, I hadn't needed to buy a second coat.

So Theo came home. I wondered, with somewhat bitter amusement, whether the neighbours realised I'd had twins. Of course they hadn't, I barely felt like I'd had twins myself. With no overlap between my identical boys, how on earth would anyone know there were two of them?

And then there they were. It finally happened, the thing that I had almost stopped believing in; both my babies came home. In the end, there was no grand fanfare, this time it just happened. Theo and I arrived at the hospital to visit Felix just after the consultant's ward round. The team had had a good look at Felix and decided he was well enough. A few calls to organise Danny to bring the car and some outdoor clothes for Felix; a quick check on our supplies of milk and suction catheters and we were ready. We said goodbye to all the Galaxy staff for what felt like the thousandth time and then we all went home.

Because of all the delays and uncertainty surrounding the twins' discharge, the home carers that had been trained up as our support had been redeployed elsewhere. This meant that we would be without any help at home for the first week or so. I was actually quite pleased; the fact that we had come so very close to losing Theo when he was in the care of a home nurse had (fairly or unfairly) done little to assure me of their competence and, more to the point, having waited so long to be together as a family, I was looking forward to being alone with my husband

and children. Since Theo and Felix were born we'd had almost no privacy; our family life had been relentlessly scrutinised. Now we needed to be left alone, to regroup and to simply get on with being a family.

> '*At long last, the Shisler clan were all together under one roof. Felix came home from hospital today to join his very grateful mummy and daddy and rather less grateful brothers and sister.*'

I hoped that this time we would get to keep everyone together for a little longer than our last attempt. One unfortunate result of the twins' recent separation was that they would no longer sleep together in the same cot. Our temporary solution was to have Theo in the cot and Felix in Evie's old basket while we tried to work out how on earth we were going to squeeze another cot in. Despite the squish (or maybe even because of it) I was absolutely bursting with happiness at having them home. It was wonderful going through the bath and bedtime routine with them all and, in the end, all three little ones got to stay up rather late as Danny and I found it too hard to resist their lovely smiles. I knew how important it was to have a routine and, usually, I am a stickler for early nights and properly enforced bedtimes, but we had waited so long for this it was inevitable that we would want to savour it.

Evie had graduated to calling them Fee-O and Fee-Lo, which was a slight improvement on Fee-O and Fee-O. Despite my hopeful theorising, she certainly did notice that her brother had doubled, and was more than a little put out about it. She spent a large part of that first afternoon trying to persuade me to put one of them to bed ('Fee-O go nigh-nigh mummy'). Overall though, I was pretty impressed by her handling of the situation, given she was little more than a baby herself. Funnily enough it turned out to be Theo who was the most jealous of Felix's return. Every time he saw me cuddling his twin he started to sulk which, naturally, just made me laugh. Fortunately, his resentment didn't last very long and, by the time they had their bath, they were friends again, and as besotted with each other as they'd ever been.

The babies' doctors had told us to expect more hospitalisations over the coming months but we hoped that it wouldn't happen for a while, and certainly that there would be nothing as dramatic as we'd been through with Theo. Despite the doctors' warnings, I couldn't help but hope that they were wrong and that, somehow, we would be able to avoid hospitals and germs and keep the babies at home for the rest of the winter.

For the next five days I was a mother of four. For five whole days I juggled bath times, changed dozens of nappies, sterilised bottles and sang nursery rhymes. I negotiated the twin buggy through the supermarket, put tiny little mittens on even tinier little fists, nagged about homework and read stories. I revelled in the ordinariness of my day; it felt an incredible luxury after the event-packed previous six months. The woman who, all those months ago, had written a letter filled with anger and fear to a bunch of strangers in cyberspace was long gone and I had discovered that there were, indeed, worse things than having three children in the space of a year.

Felix and Theo cut their first tooth – within an hour of each other – and their reactions to this new experience said everything about the differences in their characters. Whilst Felix complained noisily and chewed on his fingers until they were sore, Theo, my sweet little uncomplaining Theo, beamed and beamed and barely noticed his new toothy status. I was finally a mother of twins: I could marvel at all the funny little twin quirks and share the daily banter on the Twins List. I was, at long last, in the club. What I had learned, above all, since the boys had been born was to value an ordinary life. I would never again take it for granted; normality was a gift, a privilege even. For so many people in the world, for so many different reasons, life is a daily struggle; far too many people live in almost constant crisis. I had only been given a little taste, but it was enough to make me value dullness and predictability.

I'm grateful that I had learned to savour the present and to appreciate the life I'd been given because all too soon it was over, and Danny and I were back up to our necks in chaos and crisis. But, for five days it was just me, Danny and the kids at home together, and we relished every gloriously mundane moment of family life.

I have a photograph of Felix and Theo, taken at home during those five days. They have just had their bath and they're wearing matching plaid flannel pyjamas (Felix in red, Theo in blue), lying side by side and smiling. Two little freshly washed faces and newly combed heads, they look so lovely together and, even though Theo has oxygen tubing taped to his face, they seem to glow with wellness. Those days are like a jewel; beautiful, rare and complete. A gift we were given, a dream come true, memories to shine forever. It's not much I know, but it's something; and I'm glad we had it, a time that we can look back on, without regret, and smile.

* * *

It started in the early hours of Wednesday morning. Felix woke up snotty and miserable. Danny held him while I suctioned deep in his nose and throat, trying to clear the seemingly endless gunk, praying for him to get better to no avail. By around six o'clock it was apparent that he needed more help than we could give him at home and so, with very heavy hearts, we called an ambulance. Just five days after being discharged, he was back on Galaxy ward, back on intravenous antibiotics and utterly miserable. The following morning, almost exactly twenty-four hours later, Danny and I went through an identical process with Theo. We were back to square one, with both of them in the hospital, and with no real idea of when they'd be coming home.

I think we were more depressed than upset. After seven months of ups and downs, we were running out of emotions. I tried to be accepting; this was going to be a feature of our life for the foreseeable future. I needed to learn to pace myself emotionally. It hit me that, not only was Felix and Theo's childhood slipping away, but so was Evie's and Joey's. I felt sick with guilt when I thought about how preoccupied I'd been, especially for Evie who was still a baby herself really. It wasn't just the kids either. Danny and I were as close as ever, closer actually, but there'd been precious little fun in our relationship for as long as I could remember. It wasn't that I was worried about my marriage, but I knew we needed to devote a little time to it, and to ourselves, if it was going to stay OK. Our life as a family had been on hold for months and every moment had been steeped in uncertainty: something really had to change. I wanted to make sure that when Felix and Theo finally did come home, there was a happy and functional family waiting there for them.

The babies themselves were poorly, but I'd definitely seen them worse. They clearly had some sort of bug and Felix, as the scrawnier of the two, was in marginally worse shape than his brother. The night after admitting Theo to hospital, Danny and I were awoken by the phone ringing. Felix had taken a turn for the worse, they were looking for an intensive care bed for him, and an ambulance had been called. I can't drive (a consequence of having lived in the centre of a city all my life) so Danny pulled on jeans and a sweater and went to the hospital. I went back to sleep. Does that sound heartless? You are probably wondering how I could sleep when my child was seriously ill and being rushed to intensive care, but we had been through this so many times and I had lost count of the number of PICU admissions the babies had gone through. Danny would be with him all the time and then he could sleep once he got home, but I would have to get up with Evie and Joey in the morning. There was absolutely no point in me being awake; there was nothing I could do tonight and I would need to be fresh tomorrow. So, with the promise I had made earlier to consider the needs of *all* my family, I turned over and went back to sleep.

Danny got back at around eight the next morning, looking grey and drawn and exhausted. It had taken the hospital some time to find an intensive care bed for Felix; it was now November and the flu season was kicking into top gear. Great Ormond Street had been full and so Felix had ended up in south London, at Guy's Hospital. While Danny slept off his broken night, I made arrangements for a babysitter for Evie and then headed up to Guy's to see Felix. Having the boys in different hospitals so far apart was just another layer of complication and difficulty.

I popped in to see Theo first. He was doing OK; snotty but reasonably cheerful. We had a little cuddle but I couldn't stay with him long; I needed to get to Felix as soon as possible. It felt strange arriving at Guy's. Over the past few months I had spent a huge amount of time in hospitals, but it had been in familiar places where I knew everyone, and they knew me. The wards at UCH and Great Ormond Street had become our second home, the staff our extended family. The intensive care unit at Guy's was unfamiliar and disconcerting. After the spacious and thoughtfully designed PICU at Great Ormond Street, it felt cramped and chaotic. Felix was heavily sedated and on a ventilator; a nurse bustled around him efficiently but I couldn't help noticing that the tender love that we'd got used to seeing was missing from his care. Of course, this nurse didn't know him, or me. To her he was just another sick kid, bussed in overnight, who'd probably be gone in a day or so. I felt uncomfortable and out of place. Felix was out of it and there was no friendly face for me to talk to. My mother arrived and, after another few kisses for my unconscious baby, we decided to go back to see Theo together.

Theo was asleep when we got there. I gave him a kiss and he stirred slightly, and opened his eyes. Seeing me there, he gave me a beautiful little smile and then went back to sleep. Having seen that both my boys were settled, and realising that I could easily spend the rest of the day bouncing between hospitals, I decided to take up my mother's offer of a walk around the shops. It would, she insisted, be good for me to do something for myself, to take a little break. She was right, of course, and an afternoon of shoe-shopping or something equally fluffy would be a much-needed tonic. It had been desperately hard for my family, watching me go through so much trauma and unable to take any of the burden from me. My mother worried not only about Felix and Theo, her grandsons, but she was also filled with maternal concern for me. Since the boys had been born, all of my family, but especially my mother, had divided up visiting duties so that I could spend time with Evie and Joey. She had taken them for overnights and week-end stays, had been trained in the babies' care and in addition to this, my mother had also kept a close eye on both mine and Danny's well-being. She was the one who had ensured that Danny and I took time to go out to dinner occasionally, and that we had time alone. She had sent me for massages and manicures; anything to make sure I spent a few hours recharging my batteries from time to time. Now, seeing that I was again close to breaking point, she was urging me to step away from the drama for a little while, and I gratefully agreed.

I didn't dare to admit how utterly crushed I felt by the situation. Felix was extremely ill and there was a good chance that Theo's infection hadn't 'peaked' yet. We were as far away from home as we'd ever been; it was very hard to bear and I was afraid that, if I acknowledged the degree of disappointment I was feeling, I would be overwhelmed and unable to function. I remembered a line from a song that seemed apt and, for the rest of the day, Smokey Robinson's *I Second That Emotion*, and especially the line *'a taste of honey's worse than none at all'*, played repeatedly in my mind.

For the fourth morning running Danny and I were woken by the phone ringing, sometime before five. Danny answered, but with both boys in hospital it was clearly not going to be good news; the only question was which twin had taken a dive. It turned out to be Theo: he needed to go to intensive care. After a brief moment on the phone, Danny got up and started throwing on clothes. I didn't want him to go, what was the point? Let the hospital deal with it this time.

'Don't go,' I said.

'No,' replied Danny, 'it sounds bad.' I got up as he left; the phone rang again. It was the hospital, wanting to know if someone was on their way. I told them Danny would be there soon. The nurse sounded awful.

'Is he going to be all right?' I asked.

'We're doing everything we can.' And then she hung up.

The grey dawn was breaking over London and the world was somehow different. Everything was still and silent. The room throbbed slightly with each beat of my heart, each pulse sending out ripples across the city morning. Ripples that found my children sleeping, their hearts radiating an answer to my own. Gossamer-fine, an invisible connection from my soul to theirs. Across the roofs and silent stone and there was Felix, a tiny echo from my son. From just upstairs I felt the life of Joey and Evie, peaceful, oblivious. Where was Theo? Where was the flutter of his heart? I couldn't find it.

I sat at the computer and played a game of patience; doing deals with God or the Devil. 'If I get this out, he'll be OK'. I got it out, and then I dealt again. The phone rang. Danny's voice, breaking, told me the thing I already knew.

'He's gone.'

~ 14 ~

Death is so final. How did I not know this before? So brutally, irreparably uncompromising; no second chance, no room for manoeuvre; finished, done, dead. The silence was deafening, a roaring emptiness, a chasm as the world fell away from me. I stood on a mountain, screaming my pointless anguish into the void.

I remember the stillness. And in this vast empty space that was the world without Theo, the life in me felt clattering and clumsy and hyperreal.

Danny was coming to get me; he would be here in minutes. I called my mother, her answerphone clicked on just as she answered, her voice still blurred by sleep.

'I'll call again,' I said, and hung up; I didn't want the machine to record the terrible words I had to say. I dialled again and she answered immediately, now wide awake. She knew. Of course she knew, in those few moments between my first and second call, she had seen everything, understood everything, and all she needed now was a name.

'We've lost Theo,' I told her and I knew that she was falling and falling, just as I had, away from the world. A wave of guilt washed through me for the terrible pain that I knew she would have to bear.

I was very calm. I went upstairs to wake Joey; he would have to look after Evie until my mother and Pierre arrived. He absorbed the news in mute shock but I had no time to deal with his emotions. Danny arrived; I met him as I was coming down the stairs. He let out an awful sob and we embraced briefly but all I could think was 'not now'. I needed to get to Theo, I needed to be with him, and everything else could wait.

It didn't take long to get to the hospital; it was a journey of only five minutes or so under normal circumstances but now, in the traffic-free November dawn, we were there almost immediately. Theo was in a side room. Alan, the nurse who had been with him when he died was holding him in his arms, rocking him gently and crying. I took my boy; he was still warm.

'Oh Theo! Oh my darling, now what have you gone and done?' I kissed him and kissed him, loved him and rocked him, and I felt, really *felt*, my heart break. The sadness was awesome, humbling; it crushed everything, every thought, every feeling; forcing the breath from my body, paralysing my soul. Danny went to collect my mother while I held our baby boy and poured all my love into his still little body.

My mother's grief-etched face was almost more than I could bear. She crumbled as she took her grandson from my arms, broken with sorrow. I watched her holding him: she looked so frail, so vulnerable, almost childlike, sadness stripping away the experience of a lifetime. My mother, always so strong, so unafraid; she had no fight for this.

Danny held him and wept. He kissed his son: how would I stand it? I had never known a man more wonderful or natural as a father, a man so clearly born to the role. Watching my husband with his children had brought me such joy; it was so unfair that he should have to bury a son when there were men who walked away from their children, or killed their souls with indifference, or worse... I took Theo in my arms again. He was getting cold and I, instinctively, pulled the blanket a little closer around him. The nurse came in to take him; it was time to say goodbye and I had no idea how to do it. I handed him over and kissed him, and then he was gone and I heard a terrible cry, animal-raw, ugly and bleeding and I knew that it came from me.

We had to tell people. Danny called his parents and siblings and I wrote to the Twins List.

'Sadly we lost our darling Theo at 5.20 this morning. His heart just stopped beating and despite the best efforts of the medical staff, nothing could be done. He was seven months old and had spent just two weeks at home.

I cannot really find words just now. He was always an angel to us; we were unprepared for him to leave us in this way.

I just wanted to let everyone know.'

My brother Charlie was in New York on holiday. The first flight he could get on was not until the following day and I know he spent a traumatic twenty-four hours, far away from the rest of us, desperate to get home, grieving and alone. Even now, all this time since Theo died, Charlie gets anxious when he leaves the country, worrying that something terrible will happen at home and he will be trapped abroad again.

Nothing prepares you for this. To have to bury a child feels so against the natural order of things: our children are supposed to bury us; and then, of course, there was our uncertain religious status. Usually when someone dies, religion comes to the fore. It's not even a theological issue; it's a practical one. As the world of the bereaved shatters from loss and grief, religion provides a template, a map that leads you through the dark days and guides you back into the light. Bewildered and blinded by sadness, the traditions of funerals, shivas, wakes, ritual prayers and pilgrimages all serve the same purpose: to guide, step by step, the feet of the living until they are able to get their bearings again. Danny and I had none of this to fall back on; we would have to plot our own path.

As it turned out, this was actually a blessing. It gave us something to focus on during those first days and it allowed us to create a service that remembered and celebrated our son in the way we wanted. We went back to the Unitarian Chapel where we had married but we also asked a liberal Jewish rabbi to contribute to the service. Danny would sing a Hebrew mourning prayer; I would give Theo's eulogy; we would say goodbye to our son in a way that was meaningful for us.

I had to take clothes to the morgue, a last outfit for him to wear and anything else I wanted him to have. A few weeks earlier I'd bought some matching outfits for Evie and the twins, two pairs of little trousers and a dress, but I had never been able to get them all together to dress them up and now, of course, I never would. I took Theo's trousers, a little shirt and the sparkly shoes that Tracy had made for him, as well as his favourite stuffed toy and a little ball of pink raffia that he, for some reason, loved to play with. I wanted to see him again, to say goodbye properly. I didn't feel like I had managed it on the ward the morning he died. My brother Charlie, now back in England, came with me so that he could see his nephew one last time. My father was there too but I couldn't connect with him at all. This terrible loss had sliced though all the layers of politeness and habit, to throw a spotlight on the utter absence of intimacy between us; I no longer had the energy to pretend that he felt like family. We were shown into a little room and then they brought Theo in, lying in a Moses basket, and we stroked his little hand and kissed his cold, cold head and I don't know how I managed not to scream.

On the day of the funeral Danny and I travelled in the hearse with Theo's tiny white coffin. I remember that I talked to my baby for the whole journey, words of comfort and reassurance because he had never really been anywhere before and I didn't want him to be frightened. And I stroked the smooth wood with one hand, whilst holding tight on to my husband with the other.

The chapel was full to bursting, every seat was taken and people stood in the aisles and at the back. Our wedding had been just thirteen months earlier; thirteen months before, I had seen these self-same faces beaming at us, reflecting the joy that we felt, celebrating our perfect life. Now, it could not have been more different; our friends and family gathered to mark our loss. The room was steeped in sadness. Danny's family were there this time, all except his father who was forbidden to enter a church by Jewish law; but even he had sent a letter, to be read out during the service, that was filled with love and compassion for both of us. Danny and Charlie carried the little coffin into the chapel together, and I think most people began to cry then, because it was such a heart-breaking sight.

I didn't cry. I remained dry-eyed throughout the service; the outpouring of love and support for Danny and I was so immense, and so incredibly heartfelt, it carried me through and I was immeasurably grateful for it. I cracked only at the cemetery, as our son was lowered into the frozen November ground, and I knew that now it truly was goodbye.

We must have done the funeral right, because afterwards I could no longer feel Theo's spirit close to me. Immediately after his death, Danny and I were both acutely aware of his presence around us; I could even feel the echo of his little fingers on my face, and it seemed as if he was carrying us through those first days. But afterwards there was silence and I knew that he had gone. That night Earth passed through a vast meteor shower and, while we slept, hundreds and hundreds of shooting stars streaked across the sky. It seemed the heavens danced with fire and light and welcomed home one of their own.

As well as the trauma of Theo's loss and all the practical issues involved in getting his funeral organised, we were desperately worried about Felix. He was still in Guy's intensive care unit and was clearly very poorly indeed. The day after Theo died Danny and I went up to visit him with my mother and my father, who had flown back to England for the funeral. Felix was unconscious and on a ventilator. He looked pitifully small and frail, dwarfed by the huge machines around him. Each time his sedatives began to wear off he would become very distressed, thrashing around and crying; I couldn't help but think that he knew his twin had gone. Of course he did, how could he not? Just as I had felt the earth shift as my son's light went out, so I was sure that Felix had felt it too. His sadness scared me: what if he decided to follow his brother? The nurses at Guy's were sympathetic but they didn't know us and they didn't know Felix, and I was terrified that they would let him slip away from me.

Danny kept his arm around me as we left the hospital, although I'm not sure if it was for my benefit or for his. As we headed to the car I looked back and there was my mother; my father was with her, and they were both crying. I suddenly remembered the day, not so long before, that they had been together in the street when I broke the news that I was expecting twins. That day they had laughed together, cracking up on the pavement, giggling like children at this ludicrous turn of events. Everything had changed since then. That bright and hopeful summer had become this bleak and desperate November. Then I had been terrified of having twins but now I ached for them; my parents then had laughed and laughed together, and now they wept. Seeing my mother crying, watching her terrible sadness, was awful; I had never felt so alone. Something inside me shifted right there, and the very last traces of child-like thinking disappeared. I was fully an adult. My mother was not able to comfort me; instead a subtle shift of roles had happened, and she was looking to me to guide her out of that desperate place. It will, I'm sure, be many years before my mother truly needs my support. She is still an active, vibrant woman, the absolute antithesis of a little grey-haired granny, and far away from elderly frailty. But it will come to her, as it does to us all; the shift from carer to cared-for comes to every parent in the end and, for us, the first seed of it was sowed that day.

My anxiety about Felix's health was hardly eased a couple of days later when I took a call from one of the Guy's doctors who really needed to do some work on her bedside manner. She told me that Felix had failed another attempt to wean him off the ventilator and that, after a couple of hours breathing unaided, they had re-intubated him. She also told me that they were planning another attempt at extubation for the following day but that if he failed again we needed to decide if we should carry on. I froze; could I really have heard what I thought I did? This was exactly what I was afraid of: with no diagnosis and a deceased identical twin, Guy's were giving up on Felix. I screamed down the phone that she was not to touch my baby until I got there; Danny and I drove at top speed to Guy's, arriving on the ward breathless and angry less than twenty minutes later. I demanded to see the doctor I'd spoken to as well as her supervisor. It turned out that she was newly qualified, a very junior doctor, and had realised her mistake when I had started screaming at her. The senior consultant who ran the PICU eventually calmed me down and I got an abject apology from the poor junior doctor who was clearly traumatised by her close encounter with parental rage. Danny and I were assured, and reassured, that they *would* use whatever means necessary to preserve Felix's life. All I wanted, by this point, was to get him well enough to return to Great Ormond Street or UCH where we knew and trusted the staff.

One of the things that helped to carry us through the days after Theo's death was the incredible outpouring from people around us. Through my regular bulletins to the Twins List there were, by the time Theo died, thousands of people following our story. The babies' names had been added to prayer chains of almost every denomination; barely a day passed without me receiving an email saying something like, 'You don't know me, but I've been hearing about your children from a colleague/friend/sister and I finally thought I would write to wish you luck and tell you that our entire family is praying for you.' So as the news of our loss rippled around the world, the emails began to pour in. Danny opened a virtual book of condolences online, and I would wake each morning to find him sitting by the computer reading all the beautiful letters that had come in through the night; knowing that in just seven months our sweet Theo had touched so many lives was incredibly comforting.

The Twins List was devastated. These people had been following my story each day for over a year; they had held my virtual hand through months of ups and downs, triumphs and disasters. They had watched as I transformed from petrified mother-to-be, to wise-cracking fat lady, then to become a devoted mother of twins. Again and again Danny and I read letters from people who had sat at their computers and wept for our son. At the funeral, bouquets from the Twins List filled the chapel and Tracy even used one of her airline employee travel passes in order to be there with us. And, as we sat in the chapel and remembered our boy, all around the world people went out into their gardens and released helium balloons with their own children so that 'Theo would have something to play with in heaven'. When a child as young as Theo dies, one of your biggest fears is that they will soon be forgotten. A baby leaves such a faint imprint on the fabric of life; it is easy to wonder if it was real at all, or just a dream. The people who wrote in their thousands to Danny and me, and the hundreds who came to his funeral, told us that Theo would be remembered, that the world he left behind was a different place to the one he arrived in.

After the funeral, after all the activity and organisation of death certificates and grave purchase, Danny and I finally had some space and some peace from which we could survey this new life of ours. I felt marked by Theo's loss in unexpected ways. It was as though 'mother of a dead child' was actually engraved on each one of my cells or, like a stick of rock, bound into the core of me. Every thought I had, every word I said dripped with my bereavement; this single event seemed to define everything I was, had been, or would ever be. I felt barren. The reality of my loss of fertility hit me fully for the first time: there would be no more babies.

Walking to the hospital to visit Felix, perhaps a week or so after Theo's funeral, I was suddenly overwhelmed by tears. I felt them rising like vomit and I was powerless to do anything but turn into a doorway and curl into myself, spewing great painful sobs and waiting for the worst of it to pass.

I was acutely conscious of how my status frightened people too. In our world today the loss of a child is perceived as being the worst pain a human being can suffer. It is not so long since infant mortality rates were such that very few families would be untouched by infant death; now, thank God, it's no longer a common life event and we are rightly shocked when children die. People tiptoed around me, not knowing what to say or do, terrified of causing me more pain with an ill-thought remark or sharp reminder of my loss. In truth their anxieties were unnecessary: no word, however clumsy, could ever make me feel worse; every acknowledgement, haltingly stuttered, was like a stroke of balm across the wound. 'I don't know what to say': I heard those words a thousand times and each person that said them thought them inadequate. They surely weren't because, after all, there really wasn't anything to be said.

Felix was finally extubated (when the tube in a patient's nose or mouth that connects them to the ventilator is removed, and they breathe independently again) at Guy's and shipped back to UCH, much to our combined relief. I thought of all the different opinions we'd had over the past seven months, all the questions about walking and eating and growth, the things a parent always asks, and I realised that all of that, those hours and hours of testing and monitoring, had crystallised into just one question: will he live? For me and Danny now, all the rest was window dressing; just please tell us that we wouldn't be burying another son.

~ 15 ~

Felix's continuing health crisis, plus the fact that I still had two children at home, meant that there was no space to indulge my grief at Theo's death. Much as I instinctively wanted to retire to a corner to cry and lick my wounds, I knew that this wasn't really an option. No matter how much we were hurting, no matter how heavy our hearts, Danny and I still had to get on with life. Mourning would have to wait: at that moment the needs of the living far outweighed those of the dead. The infection that had killed Theo might have spared Felix's life, but it had taken an awful lot out of him. He'd lost weight again and was little more than skin and bone. I noted ruefully that he was still easily able to fit into newborn-sized clothes, even though he was seven and a half months old; I wondered if he would ever reach the next size. Now the words of the doctor from all those months ago came back to haunt me: 'In the worst-case scenario, they may not survive infancy.' That had turned out to be true for Theo, and I was nauseous with fear that it would also be Felix's destiny.

So I did the only thing I could do: I put my head down, I put one foot in front of the other, and I held tight on to faith that eventually, one step at a time, I would get through this awfulness; that one day all this would be in the past.

We again started the slow climb back towards discharge, but it was hard to feel very optimistic. We couldn't even get Felix up to a reasonable weight and each episode of illness saw him lose any tiny bit of flesh he might have managed to put on between bouts. I was determined to get him home in time for Christmas. This gave us just about six weeks from Theo's death and, more importantly, it gave us something to aim for. Once again we went through the process of weaning Felix from constant monitoring, ordering supplies and connecting with the community paediatric nursing team. I hardly dared breathe for fear of knocking us off course. There were so many things that could go wrong; indeed, most things *had* gone wrong at one time or another and I had learned the hard way that giving too much weight to hope just made for a heavier disappointment. Felix made stuttering progress; not so much 'two steps forward, one step back' as 'two steps forward, two steps back, then another back, then four forward, then another three back...' It was agonising but it did at least seem that overall we *were* moving forward, albeit at a snail's pace. As we headed into the last week before Christmas, Felix was just recovering from his latest cold; it seemed that we *would* be getting him home and, naturally, we were overjoyed. We left it until the last possible moment, finally saying goodbye to the nurses in a flurry of 'Merry Christmases' late in the afternoon of Christmas Eve.

Felix had been readmitted by nine-thirty the following morning. There was a horrible inevitability about it, so much so that it barely registered as disappointment for me. I had hoped for a little bit of Christmas magic. Felix would be my own Tiny Tim, beaming as the hardened heart of fate was melted by seasonal goodwill, but no; there would be no Christmas miracle for us.

We had another half-hearted go at bringing him home a week later, for New Year's Eve, but of course that failed miserably too. And, as the rest of the planet threw itself into a millennial frenzy of excitement, all I could think was that I had never been so glad to see the back of a year in my life.

One foot in front of the other; one day at a time. It became a mantra, the only possible course of action, the only way to cope. My life, mind, memories, were now so studded with painful thoughts, fears and drama that anything other than keeping my eyes fixed firmly on the absolute here-and-now *moment* was to risk being overwhelmed with sadness. Don't look back, don't look forward, don't think. Just. Don't. Look. It's hard work. Keeping all the crappy thoughts at bay is exhausting. Like trying to manage a pitifully leaking roof in a downpour, desperately stopping holes with rags, only to see a dozen new breaches appearing in the sodden timbers. 'Being OK' became a task in itself and, looking back, I think that I was actually a little bit insane with my grim cheeriness and my determination that neither I, nor my family, would be broken by the seemingly relentless pounding that fate was giving us.

It might have been a new millennium but that clearly didn't mean that anything was going to change for us. Despite our imagining that a new year was a new start and that things would surely get better, someone had obviously forgotten to tell whichever deity was doling out lousy luck, because the year categorically failed to get off to a good start. In fact, as Felix took yet another dive and was catapulted back into intensive care at Great Ormond Street, the ongoing misery started to feel decidedly comic; if we'd had a cat, this would have been the point that it got run over. Our catalogue of bad luck had now reached such monstrously unlikely proportions that it was increasingly hard to believe that it was down to chance rather than a badly scripted black comedy. The tragedies, piled unceremoniously one on top of the other, had become absurd and, bizarrely, somehow funny. There was more than one occasion that found Danny and me helpless with laughter, giggling stupidly as our world unfolded like the demented come-uppances meted out to an eternally optimistic Wile E Coyote.

Felix's next chest infection was even more fraught with worry than usual. He was back in Great Ormond Street's PICU, back on a ventilator and being pumped full of sedatives and antibiotics, despite doctors finding it increasingly difficult to find a vein that hadn't collapsed through overuse. Our relief when he started to respond to treatment was short-lived, however, as Felix's condition seemed to worsen each time the hospital tried to take him off the ventilator. Every time they extubated him he would have twelve hours or so of doing OK, followed by a rapid slide downhill until he needed to be intubated again. It was, of course, horribly frustrating and, with still no diagnosis, it was impossible to know if it was ever going to get better. His neurologist came to see me; she wanted to do a muscle biopsy after all, despite having ruled it out just months before. Even though she felt 'sure' it would not tell us anything we didn't already know, and just confirm the results of earlier tests (which told us that the problem was neurological rather than muscular), we might as well give it a try as Felix was already sedated (and thus oblivious), just on the 'tiniest chance' it would give us some new information. I consented immediately; I'd been really disappointed that we hadn't done a biopsy on the twins during the first round of testing, although I was completely unable to articulate why I felt that way. This felt to me like a step in the right direction.

The next time I arrived at the hospital Felix had a fresh, inch-long scar on his thigh where they had taken a sliver of muscle tissue. The lab findings could take up to a week to come; meanwhile my baby remained heavily sedated, oblivious to the worry he was causing his parents. A few days later we got a message from the lab: they had found something in the biopsy. The message didn't say what it was, just that the neurologist would be coming to talk to us as soon as possible. As all this happened on a Friday afternoon. 'As soon as possible' turned out to mean after the weekend; we would have to endure two whole days of waiting and wondering to find out whether our son would live or die. I think if we hadn't been so exhausted, disorientated and scared, we would have stormed the neurologist's office, demanding information; as it was, we took it mutely on the chin, swallowing this disappointment as we had all the others. Nevertheless, our need to know was very powerful. We had accepted that we might never get a diagnosis for Felix but now, knowing that there *were* answers, the suspense was very hard to bear. Danny tried to glean what information he could from the nurses; they were cagey, it's really not their job to break news to parents, but Danny returned home having overheard someone say (he thought) 'MM'.

We hit the internet and soon found information for Myotubular Myopathy, a muscle disorder that led to profound weakness. It seemed to fit Felix: the swallowing problems, breathing difficulties, all described our son. Then we came across the name of a similar disorder, Nemaline Myopathy, and Danny yelped, 'That's it, that's it! That's what I heard!' Another search, another few clicks... Bingo!

It was the pictures that were the most astonishing. They all looked just like Felix: the similarities were startling. There on the Nemaline Myopathy website, looking out at us was our son's face. Over and over again we saw our sweet little Felix in places he had never been, wearing clothes we hadn't bought. It was uncanny and there was not the slightest scrap of doubt that our boy belonged here. We looked for more information but it seemed that this one site, set up by a man with the condition in Scotland, was all there was. We learnt that Nemaline was extremely rare, extremely variable in severity, only very slowly progressive/degenerative (if at all), and that there was no treatment or cure available for the condition. Most importantly, we learnt that whilst Felix might not be getting worse, he certainly wasn't going to get any better either. As we read and learned, it became clear that Fee's best chance for survival would be a tracheostomy; he was going to need all the help he could get.

We still hadn't been officially told of his diagnosis so, even though we were pretty sure that we had hit the nail on the head, we decided to hold off on any more planning until we had seen the neurologist.

On Monday morning we were ushered into a side room, another 'bad news suite' complete with dusty potted plant, inoffensive painting and box of NHS tissues. These rooms are actually quite startlingly neutral in style, like being plunged into a bowl of tepid oatmeal; even the sunlight that comes through the obligatorily blinded window is soft and diffused and bland. The design is clearly intended to soothe and not distract in any way from the words that are being said, but the effect is actually quite unsettling, and just adds to the feeling of other-worldliness. I wondered how many tears had been shed in this strange, anonymous little room: a bowlful? A bath full? A lake?

There were two doctors to see us, the neurology consultant and the intensivist consultant (intensivists specialise in treating patients in intensive care). The neurologist explained that yes, Felix had Nemaline Myopathy (NM), a very rare, untreatable neuromuscular disorder. She outlined what little was known about the condition, nothing that we hadn't already discovered during our internet search, and told us we had been referred to a genetics clinic who could explain to us the implications for other family members. Most importantly, she stressed that she was unable to tell us whether Felix's condition was degenerative or not, but he was already at the severe end of the scale of affectedness. What we now had to decide, and this explained the presence of the intensivist, was where we went from here.

It took me a moment to understand, but to Danny and me it was then obvious: Felix should have a tracheostomy. We now knew that his breathing issues were not going to resolve.

'Well, yes, that's one option,' she told us. One option? There was another option? Danny and I looked at each other confused, and then the realisation hit us, as she continued, 'Or we could take him off the ventilator and let him go.'

No, no, no! This was not an option. We had just buried one child; there was no way we could let go of another. The neurologist asked if we were sure we understood the full implications? Felix would, most likely, *never* come off the ventilator; it meant a lifetime of equipment and nursing; wheelchairs, monitors. It was, she told us, an exhausting life. And then came the question that even now, all these years later, I can still hear in my head, and still feel the same sad anger.

'How committed to him are you?'

What? How *committed* are we? I still wonder about that question. What were we supposed to respond? As if parental commitment is somehow variable or contingent on ease of child-rearing instead of, at least to my mind, the very definition of 'unconditional love'. ('Oh, well, we are *quite* committed I suppose; but if he's going to be *a lot* of work, well, perhaps we'd rather let him die. You see, this wasn't really the baby we ordered.') We actually remained very calm (or at least we were able to appear so) as we outlined our feelings. Our 'commitment' to our son was absolute; his diagnosis in no way changed our plans which had always been, and remained, to do whatever was necessary to get him home as quickly as possible.

Now I do understand that doctors who work in intensive care units are much more familiar with death than is probably healthy, and I also understand that a certain distance is probably necessary if one is not to be completely overwhelmed by the emotional punch of the job, but the doctor's clinical questions felt brutal to Danny and me.

Having established that we were not about to give up on our son, we were able to move on to discuss treatment options. Felix was proving extremely resistant to being weaned from the ventilator; he had been intubated via his nose for weeks now and clearly couldn't go on like that. His face was covered with tape to hold the tube in place, moving him was a major production and even giving him a cuddle took at least two people to do it safely. The discomfort and restrictions of the tube also meant that Felix was sedated for much of the time; liberating him from his medical prison was a real priority. A tracheostomy, allowing him to be ventilated from his throat and without being intubated at all, seemed the best option. The doctor wanted us to take some time to think, to make absolutely sure it was what we wanted. Did we realise that our son would probably be on a ventilator for the rest of his life? Yes, yes we did, we knew all that and we knew our own minds: we were absolutely, positively in this for the long haul. Felix Samuel Shisler was our beautiful and beloved son, and we were committed.

We managed to convince the doctors that we both fully understood the implications of giving Felix a tracheostomy; and that we were not then going to leave them with a severely disabled child to support. (This had actually happened at Great

Ormond Street shortly before Felix was diagnosed. A family had wanted a tracheostomy for their child, but after the surgery found that he couldn't be cared for at home. The little boy was now living in the hospital. This made questions about our commitment a tiny bit easier to understand.) Felix was booked in for surgery at the earliest available time; we would only have to wait a few days to get his trach, much to our relief. Last time he had been given surgery, for his gastrostomy, I had fretted for days. It had been hard to accept the first concrete evidence of disability, and I was frightened and saddened by the implications of the operation, even though I knew that it would help protect the babies and their fragile lungs. This time, though, there was no such equivocation. Losing Theo had shown us, with absolute clarity, just how vulnerable Felix was. The tracheostomy would make him safer and, hopefully, keep him with us. It was categorically A Good Thing and I could hardly contain my impatience to get it done.

I was waiting by his bed for him when he came out of surgery. He was, of course, unconscious but I was so delighted to see his little face, free from tapes and tubes at last. The nostril that had held the ventilator tube was three times the size of the other one, giving him a comical appearance that the nurse assured me would not last. I must have given him a hundred kisses; despite his mismatched nostrils he looked beautiful to me, and even the trach, still fresh and bloody, wasn't too bad though I'd braced myself to be upset or shocked at the sight of it. As I sat beside my sleeping baby, watching and stroking him peaceably, I realised something: my maternal alarm bell, that instinctive knowledge that your child is hurt or in danger, was silent. For the first time since my boys had been born, it had stopped. For more than nine months the nagging sense of disquiet had never gone away, not even for a minute. It had got to the point where it no longer felt like worry, it was just part of me, a thread of anxiety that ran through everything I did, every day; sometimes it was more present and obvious than at other times, more demanding of my acknowledgement, but it was always there. Until now. I looked again at my son. We were still a long way from going home, but we *would* get there, and I knew that this time we truly had turned the corner.

My instinct was right on the nail again. Post-surgery there was an immediate and dramatic upswing in Felix's condition. My tiny boy, who was still fitting into some of his newborn-sized clothes, began to grow. A lot. Suddenly it was horribly clear just how much of his energy had been taken up with fighting for each breath. After all these months of watching his line on the growth chart beetling along flat against the bottom of the graph, it suddenly took an almost perpendicular turn as Felix squashed nine months' worth of growth into around six weeks. He looked as though we were inflating him, balloon-like, so rapid was his increase in size; he started to level out again only once he hit the fiftieth percentile line; our tiny little scrap of fragile baby turned out to be absolutely bang-on average-sized.

The struggle to breathe hadn't only affected Felix's growth; with every scrap of energy spoken for, there was nothing left for his intellectual development. Now though, we were seeing new skills every day; Felix was alert and aware and absolutely brimming with life and charm. It felt incredible and miraculous: winter was coming to an end, spring was in the air and we, at last, *genuinely* had reason to feel optimistic. Despite the severity of his disability, and despite the bleakness of his prognosis, it really did feel as though things were looking up. At least we knew where we were going now, and we could make sense of this bizarre situation; it is hard to fight an enemy that you cannot even see.

I joined the Nemaline email list, a tiny group with just a handful of families, a big change for me after the thousands-strong Twins List. I introduced myself online and found a small number of other parents of Nemaline children. A couple of the kids had a milder form of NM than Felix, and just one was more severely affected: a little girl in America called Marie, who was a few months younger than my boy and who had no movement at all. I was still subscribed to the Twins List, even though I no longer had twins, and I was still sending daily updates. I had considered leaving the group when Theo died but it didn't feel right to do so. There were so many people following our progress, praying and hoping for things to improve, I felt it would have been wrong to abandon them now, just as things were finally looking up. I knew I would have to leave the list one day, but I resolved to wait until I got Felix home. That was our goal; it always had been and these friends who had walked with us every step of the way deserved to see us get there.

Danny and I began to educate ourselves about NM: after so many months of impotence, it felt good to be able to do something useful. Now though, with Felix coming home on a ventilator, his discharge from hospital was going to be much more complicated, and it was going to take time. Although we were disappointed that there would be yet another delay to the grand homecoming, we appreciated finally being able to relax and to plan calmly and coherently, rather than on the fly.

At least there would be no more panicky ambulance dashes between hospitals; Felix was to stay in Great Ormond Street until his discharge. The hospital has a long-term ventilation ward: the transitional care unit (TCU) where children like Felix can stay whilst the complex arrangements for their home-based care are sorted out. It's a small unit, just five beds, and many of the children who pass through it spend upwards of a year there so, unsurprisingly, there was no bed for Felix available immediately. It meant that he would have to stay in the PICU in the short term. It was hardly ideal but after all the turmoil we'd been through, it didn't upset us unduly: we were making progress.

You'd think that by this point I would have learned to expect the unexpected, wouldn't you? And that I would know better than to allow myself to think that we were through the worst. But with all my energy concentrated on our children, I was really only peripherally aware that other members of the family were also having problems. And so, when Danny phoned me in the street and I heard the pain in his voice, my heart and blood froze.

'I've got some bad news,' he said, and there it was again, the crackle of emotion in his words. And then, almost immediately, before even the shape of a fear had begun to form in my mind, he said, 'Simon's dead.'

~ 16 ~

The rush of relief I felt on hearing that it was not Felix who was in trouble lasted just milliseconds before the reality of the loss of my brother-in-law took over. Danny was on his way home, I would see him there. My first concern was for my husband; he had been really close to his brother, although our recent dramas had meant they had seen very little of each other. How was he going to manage another huge loss on top of all he'd already been through? As I hurried home the ghastly awfulness of this latest twist of fate started to hit me: how could this be happening to us again? It didn't seem credible that one family could be hit so hard and so often.

My own emotions were hard to discern. With a heart that was already torn and bleeding and a constant backdrop of grieving and tearfulness, it felt like there was nowhere left to go. I had got on well with Simon from the first time I met him. He accepted me completely and unreservedly, the only member of Danny's family to do so, and I would always be grateful to him for that. But I simply had no more sadness left in me, not at all. My heart and soul ached with loss, for myself, for my husband and for his family; my tears for Simon ran into the deep river of grief that was already streaming through each day, and were lost in its churning waters.

It seemed that Simon's death was a horrible accident. He'd been suffering from depression and anxiety for some time (the panic attack on the day of our wedding was symptomatic of his illness) and had recently been put on new medication by his doctor. He'd tried a number of different anti-depressants but had problems tolerating most of them, finding that they increased, rather than lessened, the anxiety they were supposed to help. Whether the new medicine would have eventually helped, we will never know. Simon broke the first rule of anti-depressant drugs: he combined them with alcohol. He fell asleep one night beside his girlfriend; the next morning, she woke up and he didn't.

Simon was one of those people who, to me at least, always lent some credibility to the theory of reincarnation. You sometimes hear people talking about 'old souls', often in regard to babies or young children. They will tell you that their child seems to possess a wisdom born of something other than experience as if, in fact, they have been here before. Strangely, you never hear people talking about the other end of the scale, the 'young souls', and yet it seems to me that the world is full of them. Simon was a young soul I think. He seemed to find it difficult to understand how to just *be* in life, flitting from path to path, trying to work out how to be happy. If the Dalai Lama is just one death away from getting off the treadmill altogether, Simon had only just got on and was still trying to find his footing. I think he would have found it eventually, but fate intervened and took him before he'd had a chance to steady himself; another light snuffed out too soon.

Danny seemed shell-shocked, he was struggling to comprehend what had happened. His mother called: she and Danny's father were on their way to London, to our house in fact, and they would be with us in an hour or so. Even this, the fact that Rabbi Shisler was coming to see us at home, just added to our sense of bewilderment. It seemed as though all the usual rules of life had been suspended; we were now in a parallel universe where anything could (and probably would) happen.

When Danny's parents arrived, their obvious pain was the key that finally unlocked my own. These people had just lost their son. I knew what that felt like, and I was filled with sadness, as well as the compassion of recognition, for them and for all of us. I wanted to help: this wasn't the time for family arguments or recriminations. I asked what I could do; I would be there if required, or I would stay right out of things if they preferred. Did they want Danny to stay with them? If they needed him without his wife and children I would understand, whatever would make things easier for them. My only concern at that moment was that nothing I did should add to their distress. What did they want from me?

Danny's parents were quite clear: I must no longer be estranged. I was to come to the funeral and then I would sit shiva with the family. I think that, in the face of so much loss, the need to gather all remaining family together was just too overwhelming for any of us to ignore. This was still a huge step though: Danny's father was a religious leader, a much-loved and respected man who, along with his wife, was deeply embedded in the fabric of British Jewry. By having me at the shiva, I would be introduced to a vast section of the Jewish community in one go. Short of taking out a full-page ad in the *Jewish Chronicle*, it is hard to see how I could have been more publicly announced.

It's strange how things turn out sometimes. How many times had I prayed for Danny and his father to find some common ground? Now, within the space of just a few months, they had both lost a son; there could hardly be a worse place to meet.

The funeral was very hard. Not only was losing Simon incredibly sad, but the day ripped open the wounds from Theo's death that had barely begun to heal. Danny's sister Abi and I each took one arm of Danny's mother as we walked across the frozen winter cemetery. There were hundreds of people there; my in-laws are hugely loved by their community and Simon was also a well-known, popular and charming young man, impossible not to like. All funerals are sad, but there is a particular poignancy when you are marking the loss of a young life. Dozens of people were introduced to me, offering condolences for Simon and, in many cases, for Theo whose death (and indeed life) they had only just been made aware of. I was grateful for the acknowledgement.

Immediately the funeral ended, in accordance with Jewish tradition, we drove to my in-laws' home in Bournemouth for the shiva. My introduction to Jewish life and community was intense. The shiva is the seven-day period of mourning that follows a Jewish funeral. During this time, the immediate family are confined to the house while other members of their community shop, cook and clean for them. The home of the bereaved also becomes the focus of daily prayers and a great deal of activity, as friends, relatives and neighbours come to offer condolences and pay their respects. For seven days the family receive a stream of visitors, and for seven days they talk endlessly about the person who has died, sharing memories with each person who comes. By the end of the shiva, most people will be ready to move into the next stage of grieving, having been carried through the most intense stage by their community. For me it was a crash course in Jewish custom and culture, whilst simultaneously being introduced to everyone from distant cousins to the Chief Rabbi. A couple of days into the shiva, and at my father-in-law's request, I went to collect Evie from my mother's house and then returned to Bournemouth with her. Of course, she took her first meeting with her grandfather in her stride, the significance of the occasion going straight over her little head, but the rest of us knew what we were witnessing. While nothing would stem the sense of loss and grief for Simon and Theo, we at least had this glimmer of happiness, a little sparkle of joy that had been born out of all the sadness. Danny's parents had lost their son, but they had gained their grandchildren. It could not heal the hurt, but it was at least a little balm upon the wound.

A few days later, just before we were to return to London, I went out and bought two sets of children's crockery for Evie (in a kosher house you need one for milk and one for meat) as well as a toothbrush and some bubble bath. I wanted to leave them behind when we went home; my promise to Danny's parents that we would come again, soon, and bring their granddaughter. They were utterly besotted with her; their grandparental feelings were finally allowed to flourish, and it was truly lovely to see. Despite the terrible sadness that had brought about this reconciliation, and that still permeated every moment, the delight on all sides was so powerful and infectious, it brought a real sense of wonder.

Back at home I was starting to worry about something else. I had written to the Twins List about our latest catastrophe and was now really concerned that people would think I was a fantasist. Even I was having a hard time believing that one person could be so unlucky. Since joining the group at four months into my pregnancy, I had been through a cancer scare, been advised to have a very late abortion, had a baby rushed straight to intensive care at birth, had several emergency dashes to hospital with the other baby, undergone a hysterectomy, watched more testing and probing of my children than I had ever imagined possible, dealt with a child in full respiratory loss at home, lost a child, had another diagnosed with a severe, incurable, disabling condition and now lost a brother-in-law. And Felix was still only ten months old. Despite the fact that it was just my own paranoia, rather than anyone questioning my genuineness, I wrote to Linda and Tracy, the two Twins List mothers who had actually met me and my babies, asking them to confirm publicly both my existence and my story.

Hard as it was for me to process another death, it was infinitely harder for Danny. My husband's earliest memory is of meeting his baby brother. He remembers being lifted on to the bed where his mother held newborn Simon in her arms; and Danny, then just two years old, worrying because he still had his shoes on, which he knew wasn't allowed. His first memory: Simon. There from the start, two boys so very different from each other, but brothers, friends, colleagues in family life. Since the birth of the twins there had been more distance between them, as both were wrapped up in their own unfolding stories, but we knew it was only temporary, part of the ebb and flow of a sibling relationship. Simon, who accepted him just as he was, who shared his secrets and understood his roots, was now gone. The value of a relationship, the thread of a life woven into his own so closely it was almost invisible, impossible to quantify; taken for granted in the way that siblings always do. Danny and Simon looked after each other. Over the years there had been many occasions, especially during Danny's more reckless period, when Simon had come to his rescue. More recently, with Danny finally settled, it had been his turn to look out for his little brother, making sure he was eating properly and looking after himself. He'd bailed him out of several scrapes, nothing too serious but Simon's high-spirited nature meant that wherever he went, there was usually something that needed to be repaired, replaced or apologised for.

Inevitably, I worried that Danny would be broken by this latest loss. Having previously imagined that we had been cast in some weird black comedy, it now felt more as though the gods were toying with us, knocking us to the floor over and over again, waiting to see how many punches we could take until we simply stopped getting back up.

With hindsight it's easy to see that, for both of us, coming to terms with Simon's death was a much more complex process than with Theo's. When we lost Theo, the pain was immediate and intense; a knife in the heart leading to a pure, uncomplicated grief. Losing our baby was terrible and heart-wrenching, but the physical hole in our life was actually very small. With just seven months of Theo's life, most of which had been spent in hospital, we had little tangible evidence of him in our day-to-day existence; much of our loss was hopes and dreams for the future. The pain was terrible and hard to bear, but it was contained, complete and simple. Losing Simon was much harder to get to grips with. The relationships he had with friends and family were multifaceted, with subtle influences and connections, built over time and many situations. It really took Danny several years to fully absorb and accept his brother's death and, when I see the terrible pain my in-laws still carry, it brings a new sense of perspective to my own loss and sadness.

Becoming an accepted part of Danny's family was, especially for Danny, the silver lining hidden among the relentless clouds; the fact that it was so utterly unexpected only made it sweeter. The wall between us had been so thoroughly obliterated by the wrecking-ball events of the previous year, it really felt as though it had never been there. My in-laws' warm welcome into the family, as well as their utter delight in the grandchildren (including Joey, their step-grandson) was the absolute confirmation of what Danny had always told me: the rejection of me was not personal. We were soon paying regular visits to Bournemouth, making the most of the seaside attractions with Evie, as well as getting a much-needed break from the stress of our life in London. A few months later Danny's father accepted a new position, as minister to a Central London congregation, which meant that we would be living just a few miles from each other. I am sure this was, at least partly, in order to be near to us and, more importantly, our children. So, when Danny's sister Abi was married, not only did she have her own father conducting the service, but Evie and Felix were her adorable bridesmaid and (slightly reluctant) pageboy and I, like the rest of the family, sat proudly in the front row of the synagogue.

Despite the fact that they are technically not Jewish (Judaism passes from the mother) Evie and Felix are very proud of their Jewish roots. Evie now regularly spends Shabbat with her grandparents and thoroughly enjoys her status as The Rabbi's Granddaughter as she scuttles around the stairways and corridors of the synagogue with the other kids. She and Felix have been coming to Seder night dinners at Passover and celebrating Hanukkah for as long as they can remember; the rituals, festivals and songs of Judaism are as much a part of their world as Christmas. So, when I see their little faces sparkling with excitement as they sing the Hebrew prayers and take it in turns to light the Hanukkah candles, I get a rush of happy pride for them and all of us, that we have found a way to make this strange little cultural mix blend so seamlessly. The children don't seem to have any problem understanding the differences between cultures; indeed, they take it in their stride, consuming Purim chocolate coins and Easter eggs with equal relish. For me, with my 'smallest family in the world' background and rootless childhood, I love seeing my children so happily connected to their wider extended family. Evie is at the same primary school that her great-great-grandmother went to, almost a hundred years ago; my daughter has a sense of her own personal and familial history that I some-times envy. Judaism is so much more than a religion: it is a community and a culture, and I am immensely grateful that my children have been allowed to be part of it.

~ 17 ~

When I was twenty-one I spent some time working on cruise ships and did a number of cruises around the Caribbean before landing a job on a ship that was just starting a four-month world cruise. It was a fantastic way to see the world, and circling the globe by sea gave me a real feel for, and understanding of, how big this planet is. We sailed from San Francisco and finished up in New York; in between we visited dozens of countries, seeing the subtle shifts that made one culture become another. Most cruises will have, at most, a couple of days at sea at a time, but we had some very long crossings as we slipped between continents. We were, I think, ten days crossing the Pacific; ten days without land, of seeing the horizon as a circle around you; ten days of life entirely governed by the rhythm of the sea. And then, suddenly, you reach port and you're ashore and the strangest thing happens: you can't walk straight. After days of constant motion, solid land feels bizarrely unsteady; your 'sea legs' won't switch off and you giggle as you step on to the dockside with your drunken gait and a body that's still being rocked by yesterday's waves.

It took a while for me to lose my 'crisis legs' after everything that had happened, and to stop being braced for disaster at any moment. There was, though, a palpable atmosphere of relief and even the most cautious observer could see that things were truly starting to calm down. Perhaps it was the advent of spring that was making me feel optimistic: the warmer weather meant less nasty bugs about for Felix to catch. I had learned that for children like him, the first winter is always the biggest challenge; get them through that in one piece and their chances of survival increased massively. The first winter had been like a war zone; we had come through it battered and bloody; we had taken casualties. Theo and Simon were no longer with us; but we had survived and, miraculously, Felix had made it.

For the first time in a very long while I found myself in a position to stop and take stock of where I was. I had been so busy reacting to life, I had barely had a chance to notice the world around me. Planning ahead had been out of the question; the pace of change had been so great that trying to anticipate future options was pointless. Now, though, life seemed to have returned to a more manageable speed, and clear thinking no longer seemed like a ludicrous fantasy.

I was part of the Great Ormond Street community now; the small, elite group of parents whose children are there for over a year. Being with Felix in hospital became my 'job'. I'd get up in the morning, get Joey off to school, settle Evie with my wonderful childminder and head for the hospital. For the rest of the day I'd be with Felix before returning home to spend a few hours with Evie before bedtime. It wasn't exactly a 'normal' life, but it was the closest I'd come to one for a long time, and it actually felt pretty good.

As the weeks of the summer ticked by we started getting everything ready for Felix to come home. We've been very lucky in that firstly, we have a supportive health authority which was prepared to commit itself to Felix's care; and secondly, we live very close to Great Ormond Street, just a few minutes' walk in fact, so the hospital were able to oversee and advise on the community nursing arrangements. Posts for carers were advertised and a team was employed and trained in everything from ventilator management to basic physiology. Danny and I had to be trained in everything too: our CPR skills were updated to cover how to resuscitate someone with a tracheostomy, and we learned how to manage our son's equipment and deal with emergencies. It was strange for me, after over thirteen years of being a parent, to find myself so clueless as to how to look after one of my own children.

We moved house. Another lucky break as, against all odds, we found a flat big enough to accommodate our family (with even an extra room for Danny to work from) in the same area, so we didn't have to change hospitals or health authorities; best of all, it was all on one level with wide hallways and doors – perfect for wheelchair access. I painted Felix's room in tropical colours: lime, tangerine, fuchsia and sunshine yellow. He would have a carer around the clock once he got home; his room would be a workplace as well as a child's bedroom, so I wanted to make it comfortable for his team, as well as for him. It was hard to believe that finally, almost a year and a half after giving birth, I was actually getting a bedroom ready for Felix. I wanted it to be perfect, we'd waited so long; even the cushions on the sofa were chosen with love and attention to detail. It was really happening: my baby was really coming home!

Yet despite the continuing strides towards Felix's discharge, and the genuine progress we were making every day, I wasn't quite ready for him to come home. There were still a couple of things that I needed to do before I could really close the door on the past and step properly into the future. Since getting Felix's diagnosis of NM, and so deciding to give him his tracheostomy, he had been thriving. The improvement in every single aspect of his health was astonishing; he was barely recognisable as the same child. My scrawny, kitten-weak baby had transformed into a rosy-cheeked, chubby-fingered toddler (if that's an appropriate term for a child who can't walk). It was impossible not to wonder whether Theo could have been saved.

Hindsight is, of course, wonderfully accurate and, much as I wanted to move forward, I kept finding myself going back to decisions made in those early days and questioning the judgements of the time. The only diagnostic test for NM is a muscle biopsy; the one step we hadn't taken. When the boys left the NICU at six weeks of age, on their first day on Galaxy Ward, the consultant paediatrician had told me that she believed they had a myopathy. She pointed out their classically myopathic features (open mouth, 'sleepy' eyes, little facial expression) and immediately sent them to Great Ormond Street for tests. I didn't want to believe her, maybe it was too early or too scary but, more than anything, I wanted her to be wrong. And at GOSH they gave me what I wanted. It was *not* a myopathy they told me, no need to do a biopsy, the results would be negative. This, they felt certain, was a neurological problem. It turned out that they were wrong.

I asked for a meeting with the consultant neurologist that had made the decision not to proceed with further testing; I wanted to find out her reasoning and also put my own mind at rest, confident that we had done all we could for Theo. I wasn't looking for someone to blame, just an understanding of why certain decisions were made and, most importantly, to see that lessons had been learned from the experience. In the meeting the doctor explained that it was the results from the babies' brain scans that had led her to assume a neurological, rather than muscular, cause of Felix and Theo's condition. Although the slightly reduced myelin and tiny spots of calcium in their brains fell well within the range of 'normal' results, these things *could* also be indicative of a problem. Their muscle function tests had not shown anything (NM does not show up through this sort of testing) and these facts in combination had persuaded her in her prognosis. Furthermore, she told me that even if NM had been correctly diagnosed, it would not have made any difference as Theo's treatment would have been the same.

I was ready to accept that the brain scans were the red herring and that they led us down the wrong path, but I still don't really believe that a diagnosis would have made no difference to the way the babies' condition was managed. Clearly if we had known that Theo was not going to 'grow out of it', that he would always have respiratory problems, I have no doubt that Danny and I would have pushed hard to get him a tracheostomy, instead of leaving him to struggle for practically every breath. In the end, the neurologist told me that, despite everything that had happened with Theo, she stood by her decisions at the time and that, presented with a similar situation in the future, she would do exactly the same thing again. I know that this is the nearest I am likely to come in terms of closure and I can only hope that lessons learned from Theo's death will one day save the life of another child.

Letting go and moving on. We'd come so far and been through so much, I wanted to draw a line under everything and start again. A fresh page, a clean sheet; I couldn't bear the thought of carrying all that pain and sadness into the next stage of my life; I wanted to be able to parcel up the whole nightmare and walk away. We had a new home, a new family; we were different people from the ones who had set out on this bizarre adventure together. When we moved house, I left the barely used twin buggy behind. Felix and Theo had come to visit me in hospital in it, when I had my hysterectomy. Was that really a year ago? There had been a couple of walks but, otherwise, the buggy had never left the hospital ward. My mother had bought it for me when I was pregnant, determinedly tracking down the last one of the discontinued line I'd set my heart on. But it was a symbol of something that had gone: the twins. When Theo died, 'the twins' died too. Felix now, just like his siblings, was a singleton and I had lost my magical status as a mother of multiples. How hard had I fought against the idea of twins? I'd cried and cried because I didn't want my perfect world to change; perhaps I knew. Perhaps I could sense the future somehow, and all the sadness that was coming; or maybe I was just a fool. Whatever; I would have given everything to have my twins back again. So I left the buggy behind, closed the door on it and walked away. I shed some more tears but I knew it was the right thing to do; we were moving into our new home and our family had to feel complete. I didn't want my children to grow up in sadness, God forbid they should feel that they somehow weren't enough for me, or that there was a hole in the heart of our family. We were moving on and Theo and 'the twins' couldn't come with us.

~ 18 ~

While the first year after Felix came home was really just a blur of readjustment, things did eventually settle into a manageable state. The early months in particular had been ludicrously busy, with what felt like every healthcare professional within a ten-mile radius having Felix on their caseload, as well as a regular home visit on their agenda. A child on a ventilator at home is still enough of a novelty that my family has a certain curiosity value so, when the *fourth* health-visitor (with obligatory student in tow) 'popped by' to introduce herself and see if we needed anything, I finally cracked, tearfully shouting that the only thing I *needed* was some bloody peace and quiet. That was my turning point; I threw an assortment of bewildered nurses and therapists out of my house that afternoon, and took the first steps towards reclaiming my life. I think there were another couple of noteworthy meltdowns over that period, but I am told that I actually did pretty well compared to most families, many of whom live in a permanent fug of barely suppressed rage. It's not really surprising; there are huge life adjustments to be made when you have a child on a ventilator; almost everything you do needs to be rethought. Combine this with a sudden loss of privacy as everything about your life is scrutinised; plus the ongoing emotional fallout from having a profoundly disabled child, and it actually seems miraculous that I was *ever* calm.

So we survived the transition into this strange new life and, of course, it wasn't all terrible and stressful. It was lovely having all of us in the same place, and being able to spend time with my other children was wonderful. Most importantly, Felix was absolutely blooming now he was home. It was really quite incredible; people had told me that these children came on in leaps and bounds once they finally got home but, nevertheless, it was amazing seeing Felix change and blossom so much in such a short time. Inevitably though, it was his needs that continued to dictate much of our family life.

Even though Felix has a carer pretty much around the clock, taking him out still requires military-style planning and serious packing. Between the ventilator, battery, suction machine, emergency tracheostomy change bag (in case of blocking), hand pump (in case of vent failure), feeding kit and feed, going out was never going to be either spontaneous or simple (and all this is before you add the inevitable Power Rangers, Pokemon and Transformers which, according to Felix, are also a vital part of his kit). Over the years I have got readying Felix's 'baggage' down to a fine art; I know what is really essential for any given trip, and what is merely important; I know what is the bare minimum I can get away with and I know how to improvise. But those early days, when it was all new and far from being instinctive, and with Theo's death still an all-too-recent event, I did everything by the book, rattling through my enormous checklist and sending up silent prayers to the gods of fate.

As well as the constant stream of therapists coming to the house, we also had endless clinic appointments: neurology, respiratory, spinal, cardiac, orthopaedic, hearing... Almost no part of the human body is unaffected if you have muscular issues. There are muscles for eating, breathing, sitting, the heart is a muscle, food is pushed through the gut... I tried not to think about how scared it made me or the fact that as Felix grew, his already-weak muscles would not keep pace with his increasing weight and so, inevitably, things would get worse as he got bigger. Because of the huge variation in severity of NM, no one could tell us if Felix would ever walk or talk as he got older: we could only watch and wait and hope.

Felix, of course, has never, and probably will never, know privacy. He is never alone, watched over even in sleep and monitored for everything from temperature to mood. Nursing will be a fact of his life forever; another reason for allowing him to form his own independent relationships. One day hopefully he will, like other children, take control of his own life. He will make the decisions about his care and the way he lives in harmony with his team. The models for our life today, and his in the future, are not our parents or other families. We are learning from the experience of communes with their need to consider others, perhaps not chosen companions, in every aspect of personal life.

Grieving for Theo seemed to come in waves; it was incredibly hard knowing that he had been dead for longer than he had been

alive. I felt like he was being erased, his stamp on the world growing fainter every day. As the first anniversary of his death
approached, all my emotions intensified. Not just my sadness for
Theo, but also my fears for Felix and the guilt I felt because of
how preoccupied I'd been, and all the things I'd missed with Evie
and Joey.

On the day itself Danny and I went to his grave together. It
was a bitterly cold November day and the wind bit into my cheeks
as we walked through the cemetery. Theo's little place was under
a tree, far from the road and entrance. It was a nice peaceful spot
and I had been glad, when I first saw it, that he was somewhere
pretty but now, as we neared the grave, I just felt overwhelmed
with sorrow. I laid my flowers down and spoke to my son for a
little while, pouring out my love and grief. I wanted him so badly;
I could hardly stand to be so near to where he lay, and yet not be
able to hold him in my arms, and I was seized with a powerful
urge to dig into the frozen earth and save him, comfort him, just
to touch him. The ferociousness of the pain took my breath away:
being there was just too hard. I haven't been back to the cemetery
since that day. Maybe I will be able to again in the future, I don't
know. Whatever happens, I will be buried there myself one day, as
will Danny; close to Theo at last.

At the entrance to the Great Ormond Street chapel there is a
huge, heavy, leather-bound volume in a glass case. This book
contains the names of all the children who have died while patients
at the hospital. Each day the chaplain unlocks the case and turns
the page, to reveal the names, and ages, of the children who have
an anniversary that day. Even though he actually died at UCH,

Theo is in the book; he was still under the care of GOSH and so he qualified for an entry. Theo William Shisler, 1999 aged seven months, reads his entry. He shares his page, November the thirteenth, with four or five other children; one day the page will be full and then, I suppose, they will start a new book and another little trace of my boy will be gone. After my trauma at the cemetery on that first anniversary, I resolved to not go there again. Instead, when the day comes around, I go to the chapel, and I leave flowers and shed my tears by the memorial book. There are always flowers and cards, and even little gifts, left there; I am clearly not the only parent who comes to honour a child in this way.

It took me a long time to recover from Theo's death. Actually, I'm not sure that you ever 'get over' the loss of a child but you can learn to live with it. When it first happened, I felt defined by the loss. It was such a huge thing, such a massive event, that it felt as though everything else in my life, both before and after Theo, would now be seen through the window of his death. It took a long time for that to pass. In some ways I can see that I *am* defined by it, certainly it is one of the key events in my life and always will be, but the influence now is subtle; I no longer wear my loss on my sleeve. I loved my son more than I will ever have words to tell; my heart was truly broken when he died, but time blunts even the fiercest arrow. Eventually the day comes when it is not your waking thought, where every action is no longer filtered through the knowledge of your loss. Slowly, you recover yourself. Older and sadder certainly, but also wiser, deeper and stronger. The loss of a child puts you into a very elite 'club' and while no one would ever choose to join, it cannot be denied that membership brings certain personal changes, not all of which are undesirable.

Some people resist this process of healing, protecting their grief from the softening effects of time, holding on to the safety of the familiar. Part of me understands this: as grief wanes there is a definite sense of another kind of loss. You are 'moving on' and that means letting go of your child, allowing the memories to blur a little, letting yourself be happy without them. It is hard; when it started to happen to me, a part of me resisted. I didn't want to stop missing him, I didn't want to forget. I felt guilty, as though I was betraying Theo by not crying for him every day. At that point I understood why some families build a shrine, why they stop, frozen in their sadness, and never move on. It was not the choice I ultimately made, but I understand it.

And then I discovered the online world of miscarriage and neonatal death. Here I came across women still in active mourning for a pregnancy lost many years (and occasionally decades) earlier. Mothers who encouraged a child to think about, grieve for and even pray to their own stillborn twin. I came across huge, epic memorial websites for children who had lived for only hours, websites that must have taken months of intense work to put together, sometimes with a link at the end to a page for the living child, almost as an afterthought. I am not trying to belittle the grief of a miscarriage, particularly for someone struggling with infertility issues, but most of these women (and it is always women) had other children living. It disturbed me hugely, this fetishisation of grief and loss. It seemed that, for some people, the dead child had become the focus for every lost dream or missed opportunity in their life, the justification for all the feelings of sadness and being unfulfilled. What I gained from visiting these sites was a very clear picture of what I *didn't* want for myself. I read these heart-breaking tributes to children who had barely existed, and as I wandered through this tear-drenched world, I knew that this was never going to be the answer for me or my family.

I know that sometimes heart-break is so vast it is almost luxurious. It rips through you, laying waste to other feelings, forcing you to let go of everything else, even your own sanity. Pain, at its most acute, honed to a perfect razor-edge, slices cleanly through your life; it's like a drug as it pushes all but itself out of your mind and, like any other drug, it can be addictive, and it can be abused.

Evie and Felix don't remember Theo, they were too young when he died to understand, but they know all about him and Evie, in particular, likes to talk about her 'brother who's an angel', and wonders if he goes to 'angel school' in heaven. I have some photographs of Theo on display, as I have of all of my children; there is no denial of him, of his loss or even of mine and Danny's sadness over his death. But I want my children to know that we are a whole family today, the family we are meant to be. We *are* complete, and we have a right to be happy. The thought that they might grow up feeling as though I had never got over losing Theo, that they were not enough for me, is horrifying. As I read the stories of women who could not let go, I began to see that all the pain and sadness surrounding them must have become deeply embedded in the fabric of their families, and I promised I would not let it happen to mine. Much as I loved and missed my sweet angel, I would learn to be OK, because life belongs to the living however much we long for the dead.

As part of this, I finally signed off the Twins List. The other members of the group assured me that, in their eyes, I would always be a mother of twins and that I had a place on the list for as long as I wanted. Some people even tried to persuade me to stay but, while I was touched by their affection, I knew that it was really time to leave. It was difficult to say goodbye to a group of people who had been through such an extraordinary time with me, not least because it was another step away from the past and from Theo. But it was getting harder to read the list each day: the women I had been pregnant alongside were now writing about first steps and first words and all this could only underline how very different my life was. I had stayed until Felix came home: after all the support I'd been given I wanted my online friends to share in our eventual victory, but with that done I was just marking time, putting off my final severance from twin-hood.

The Twins List contained it all, I realised. It was there, an entity, a slice of my life. Writing to the list each day, being part of that community, it had become synonymous with drama and epic, life-changing events. I had joined the group two years ago as one person; ready for change, or so I thought. I didn't know who I had become, I didn't know where I was going, but I knew I couldn't really begin a new chapter until I'd finally drawn a line under the old one.

Somewhere around a year after we brought Felix home, I hit a huge emotional hole. I was still taking the anti-depressants I'd been prescribed just before Theo died, but they no longer seemed to be having any effect. I could feel everything in me slowing, every action getting harder, as though I was wading through an ever-thickening lake of glue. Even following a train of thought felt exhausting and pointless. I changed to a stronger anti-depressant, but it just scrambled my brain and made things even worse. I also tried going back to some AA meetings, attempting to reconnect with the place that had got me well once before, but I felt so alien and empty; the social nature of the fellowship seemed brittle and freakish. My doctor diagnosed post-traumatic stress disorder and recommended counselling, but I had neither the energy nor the motivation to get it organised and, in any case, the very last thing I wanted to do was sit around talking about my 'tragic past' with someone whom I was paying to listen to me.

I'd love to be able to say that I found some great strategy for turning things around, or that I discovered a really effective form of therapy, but the truth is that, in the end, it was simply time that made the difference. Gradually I began to pick up the pieces of myself, and rediscover some enthusiasm for life. Sometimes all you can do is allow yourself to go through the process. I learned to be gentle with myself, to accept that it would take time to absorb everything that had happened, and that grieving would be ongoing. It took about a year, maybe a little more, before I started to come out of the darkness. The depression slowly ebbed away, leaving me changed in a thousand tiny ways, and with a far deeper understanding of, and respect for, life's essentially cyclical nature.

~ 19 ~

It's funny how things turn out. Among all my wild and varied imaginings of where my future might lie, there was nothing even vaguely similar to what has actually come to pass. Of all the changes, big and small, internal and external, my family and I have had to encompass, this quantum leap into the world of special needs has been the most dramatic. With Felix home, we became a 'special family'; our place in the world shifted, and it would take time to learn the new terrain. My first task was to take a cold, hard look at my own thinking; as riddled with misconceptions and prejudices as it was, it was not a pretty sight.

The very idea of disability had always been as weird and alien to me as theoretical mathematics or stamp-collecting: it was something that simply didn't exist in my life or my consciousness. It shames me now when I realise how horribly ignorant I was. When I was growing up, segregation was the acceptable norm for people with disabilities. Some of the kids in our street, kids that I knew and played with, had a disabled brother who lived in a 'home'. His mother would visit him monthly and I remember my family being sympathetic about the terrible burden she carried. Now, of course, I am shocked by my younger self; did we *never* ask after the boy? How was it so easy for us to accept without question that an institution was the right place for this child? I don't think it ever crossed my mind to wonder how he felt, hidden away, apart from his siblings and mother. I look back and I am horrified and ashamed; my heart breaks for a little boy I didn't know and never cared about. I care now. But, of course, it's far too late.

As I slipped from childhood into adulthood, disability continued to be invisible to me. I knew in theory that it existed, I'd seen the parking spaces and the specially adapted bathrooms and, as a socialist, I'd even paid lip-service to the notion of equal rights and opportunities, but I didn't *know* any people with disabilities and there seemed to be no overlap between my world and theirs. Sometimes I would see on TV, or read about in a newspaper, a family struggling to raise their disabled child (and they do 'struggle' in the media stories; it is always hard) and I would note that I could never live like that, that I would never have the strength or patience, as if these people, these families, were somehow a different breed. They were the kind of people that these things happened to, and I was not.

Despite my liberal pretensions, my view of disability was surely as prejudiced and discriminatory as it's possible to be. I probably bought into every generalisation and cliché: people with disabilities were unstylish, uninteresting, wannabe-martyrs. Worthy and humourless, unassertive and dull of mind and, despite their absolute and obvious 'otherness', desperately ordinary. I realise that all this makes it seem as though I had a clearly formed opinion; but that would have involved me actually sparing some time to really think it through. Instead, I tossed my lazy ideas into a corner of my mind and got on with the rest of my life. I'm glad, in some ways, that I've been such an appalling snob; it certainly helps me to understand what my son is up against. I'm not proud of the fact that it was necessity, rather than conscience, that changed my perspective; but at least I know, and from personal experience, that prejudice can be deeply entrenched in even the most seemingly tolerant soul.

Of course, with Felix and Theo's arrival, I discovered the ludicrously obvious, forehead-slappingly apparent fact that disability could happen to anyone. And yes, I felt like a fool.

Perhaps though, it shouldn't be so surprising that disability is kept at arm's length: perhaps we don't want to be able to identify too closely with those inhabitants of the world, because that might make the possibility of it happening to us just a little too close for comfort. My family and I are now living proof of life's fundamental unpredictability. In this sanitised, safety-checked world most of us are shielded from life's harsher realities. Only a generation ago, loss was part of life. Every family knew what it was to lose a child; illness was serious and often life-threatening; doctors were limited and fallible. Today, at least in the developed world, miracles have become mundane. Doctors, arm-in-arm with technology, perform amazing feats and we, spoilt by so much success, expect nothing less. I have faced people's incredulity at the incurable nature of my son's condition too many times to count. So I can see that we, as a family, are now a reminder that despite the protections and the incredible advances in medicine, there are still no guarantees.

One of the legacies of a society that keeps people with disabilities at arm's length, that houses and educates them separately, is fear. I was certainly afraid. The little snatches of disabled life that I had been shown, the financial hardship, the backbreaking work of a carer, the lack of support, all terrified me. It is this same fear, I'm sure, that leads to countless disabled children being left in institutions. The media don't help either: when the lives of people with disabilities are portrayed as crushingly hard, and parents of children with special needs are shown as superhuman, it shouldn't really be a surprise when some families feel unequal to the task.

The mundane reality, of course, is that there is nothing special or different about parents of children with disabilities. We are ordinary mothers and fathers; some are good parents, some are not. We are no more patient or selfless than any other parents and, like most, sometimes we rise to the occasion and sometimes we don't. I found that these things *did* happen to people like me, there was no benign God carefully ensuring that only wannabe saints were chosen for this path; even the intolerant, impatient and downright flaky got picked.

It's certainly been an education. The world looks very different from behind a wheelchair and, apparently, I look very different to the world from that position too. I'm not someone who particularly stands out in a crowd these days. As a younger woman, my penchant for short skirts and high heels attracted the usual catcalls and whistles from the kind of leery men who were struggling to remain in the gene pool. Even further back, as a teenager in the punk era, I positively courted the attention of strangers, with loud clothes and even louder hair. These days, though, I barely raise a glance as I walk down the street; my showboating days are definitely behind me unless, that is, I am with Felix.

My son always stands out, wherever we go. I'm not sure exactly what it is that grabs people's attention first: maybe it's the wheelchair, or the ventilator tubing that snakes around the chair, perhaps it's his tracheostomy or even his 'myopathic features'; the muscular weakness that gives his beautiful face the stamp of disability. Most people do at least have the courtesy to try to be discreet in their gawping but some, apparently unhindered by manners, stare at my child as though he were another species.

As I began to adjust to this new life of ours, I started to see that the fallout from our status as a special needs family wasn't necessarily all bad. While it's true that it takes time, and some effort, to get to know Felix (who communicates through an entertaining mixture of signs, expressions, pointing and semi-formed word-fragments) there are real gifts for those who make the journey. Disability is a frightening and unfamiliar concept for many people; breaching that fear, being able to let go of misconceptions can be a profoundly moving experience and I have never tired of seeing people make that journey. Even more profoundly, just knowing Felix shows people a very different life perspective, and I have yet to find anyone who doesn't feel the richer for it.

Perhaps the only advantage to him of this barrier to instant rapport has been that it holds back lesser people. We have certainly found that those who see the task of getting through it too onerous, who baulk at the thought of having to make an effort to get to know someone, are people who have little to offer as friends. It weeds out the selfish, the unimaginative and the lazy with ruthless efficiency and, for that at least, I am grateful.

On first meeting, Felix's condition *is* shocking. I know this, and I understand that most people need a little time to overcome that shock. The ventilator, suction machine, humidifier, sundry supplies, monitors and batteries, all wired together and wired to him does look pretty dramatic. I sometimes forget this: I just don't see it any more, and then someone new comes along, and I see their reaction, and it reminds me that actually, for most people, this really *isn't* normal. It's funny how perception adjusts; we adapted quickly and easily, absorbing so many things that had once been utterly alien. I still see this adjustment process in people who come into our life. There is a point, maybe on their third or fourth visit, when all the technology and all the wires shift from being Felix's most obvious and striking feature, to become an almost invisible backdrop, and then they see him: just a kid. I watch people relax as they recognise the familiar territory and orient themselves once again, and I see something else too: a tiny step away from their fear of disability. It's just a drop against the ocean of prejudice that exists but, nevertheless, it's a drop of good.

Despite the fact that I knew it was a very common occurrence for families like ours, I was still surprised at the way a number of friendships seemed to simply dissolve after everything that had happened. As we started to regain some stability, it became clear that some people had simply dropped out of our life. At the time it was another shock; why, what had we done? We hadn't changed. I've had time to ponder that now, to think about what makes a person walk away from a friend in their time of crisis. In truth, I still don't really know; I hope that I would never do such a thing. But my most charitable assessment is that they did it because they were afraid. Afraid that perhaps we would be too 'needy'; that we would require unmanageable levels of support; that we would not be *fun*. It is a sad fact that much of the world views our situation as tragic, even pitiful. I am astounded by the number of people who think that I am an 'inspiration' because I still manage to be happy. Happy! As though the terrible trauma of having a child with special needs precludes joy forever.

The world that I live in today is a very different place from the one I used to know. In many ways, this is a harsher world. Before I had my boys, I knew only one person who had lost a child: a family friend whose six-year-old son had been killed in a horrific car crash. The very idea of a child's death was unspeakable, terrifying and, thankfully, vanishingly rare. Now, besides Theo, I have actually lost count of the children I have known who have died. We may no longer live in a time when infant mortality affected everyone from dairymaids to duchesses, but lift the lid on this unseen community, open your eyes to our invisible land, and you will find child death lurking around every corner. Of the four children who shared TCU with Felix, two are now gone. I have seen many parents walk the path from the breath-catching, gut-wrenching, screwed-in pain of the first days, through the sad emptiness of the weeks and months that follow until the day they discover that actually they can smile again, and all the guilt and confusion that this brings.

While I have been writing this book, there have been a number of disability stories in the media. They paint a picture of how the world sees my son that, frankly, terrifies me. Terri Schiavo, the American severely brain-damaged woman whose husband and parents fought over her 'right' to live or die, finally passed away some thirteen days after having her feeding tube removed on judicial orders. In England, Jacob Wragg's soldier father ended his life in a so-called 'mercy killing': the jury was unable to decide whether this was lawful or not and so a new trial will have to take place. Two more sets of parents definitley have fought, and lost, cases against hospitals treating their children. In both cases the doctors wanted to institute DNR (Do Not Resuscitate) orders, while the parents pleaded for their children to be given a chance to live. One of these children is now dead; the other, a little girl called Charlotte Wyatt, who was massively premature, is (at the time of writing) hanging in there. In these cases the right to live versus the right to die has hinged on a perceived notion of 'quality of life'. None of the subjects themselves was able to tell us what they felt or what they wanted; the decisions, ultimately, were based on the highly subjective belief that 'I wouldn't want to live like that'. It scares me. Will someone, one day, look at Felix with his feeding-tube and ventilator and think: 'I wouldn't want to live like that?' And what if I'm not there to fight for him or, even worse, am overruled by doctors and judges who tell me that I am in denial, over-emotional, a mother who simply cannot face the truth and let her baby go?

Quality of life. Such a strange concept, this idea that we can judge a life worth living, worth fighting for, and leave to die the lesser lives of poorer quality, because we 'wouldn't want to live like that'. Strangely, we only use this argument about people with disabilities: it seems that able-bodiedness is the only quality of life that counts.

Felix has a fantastic quality of life, this much is beyond dispute. He is an extraordinarily happy child, bursting with mischief and delight. His life is filled with people who love him and, at least for now, he seems to have no issue with his inability to walk or function like his classmates. He has learned that humour is a great tool for breaking through barriers, even though it sometimes gets you into trouble at school; he is cheeky and charming, instinctively using his comic skills to put people at ease and to help them through their own, initial, discomfort. Felix's confidence and self-acceptance are infectious: he has an apparently unlimited capacity for affection, which he pours into almost everyone he encounters. Most importantly, despite the many trials of his short life, I have never detected the slightest hint of self-pity in my son. Whatever his physical problems, Felix is one of the most emotionally healthy people I have ever met.

This *is* my world now. Despite my previous prejudice and casual indifference, I belong here. The sense of community, kinship and even pride is profound. And I am still resolutely myself, tottering through the streets on illogically high heels, in brazen, open defiance of the accepted wisdom that would see all us special-needs mothers in practical fabrics and sensible flats. Against all expectations (chiefly my own) it turned out that I like it here. I like the comradely smiles I get when I pass another wheelchair-pushing parent in the street; I like the laid-back chattiness of the disabled section in the theatre, the utter absence of preciousness, the deep understanding of life's priorities and the gallows humour. And the biggest revelation of all? Amazingly, it seems that life on this side of the fence is anything but dull and conformist. All those years I thought I was being daring and edgy and now it turns out that I was really never anything but mainstream. Peering at the world from this side, I am learning how radically different perspective can really be; and the middle-aged punk-rocker in me seems to get a kick out of the shock factor.

What is hard about this life is not dealing with Felix's disability: it is dealing with the points where that has to interface with the world. Having to fight to get him all the things he needs – an education, the best equipment, the right therapy, even the key to the disabled bathroom – is exhausting; and I, with my middle-class demeanour and fluent English, get it easier than most. I know my son is perfect, but I get tired of having to tell the world this *every single day*.

For me though, the very hardest aspect of my world today is dealing with the dark seam of fear that runs through the bedrock of my life; I will never get used to that. Mostly, any fear rumbles softly in the background, a dull indefinite ache, but sometimes it lashes out, cutting a salty wound into my skin. It creeps up slowly at first, nagging at me quietly, forcing me to shout my happy, busy thoughts above it. I jam metaphorical fingers into internal ears, 'la la **LA**, I'm not *listening*!' Sometimes, though, I can't fight it any more and I have to drop the defences, letting the fear wash through me, and, after the tears, there is always a sense of relief.

On some level I suppose I am always afraid; there is so much of this life that scares me. From the prosaic fear of all the work that has to be done, therapies, arrangements, equipment, the daunting mountain of *stuff* that you can't screw up because the stakes are so high. To the darker fears: will my child be happy? Who will love him? Will he always have the tenderness, the unconditional adoration that he thrives on now? Dear God, please don't let my little one, my chubby-fingered, sticky-kissing angel, grow up to be lonely. These are my fears for Felix. My biggest terror is purely selfish. It is the thought that I may lose him. The fact is, it is always going to be more likely that I will bury Felix than that he will bury me. I have lost one child already, I know how fine and fragile is the line between life and death. I know how much it hurts, the spectre of that future-pain can sometimes overwhelm me and, even after all this time, I cannot find a way to live peaceably with this knowledge.

Felix is defined as Medically Fragile. The possibility that he will not survive to adulthood exists as the unspoken coda to his life. When I talk about his future, about what he needs to develop into a fully rounded person, I often see people's eyes flicker 'Does she know? Is this denial?' Realistic optimism, a contradiction in terms, is the position I try to maintain: realistic enough to be taken seriously, positive enough to raise expectations. It is not an easy line to walk.

Felix's poor muscles have led to a mild scoliosis (curvature of the spine) which is worsening as he grows. I desperately want to pretend it's not happening, but I look at him and I know that it is. Eventually, inevitably, he will need surgery to correct it, before it starts to crush his internal organs. Scoliosis surgery is complex and risky; the very thought of my son going through it scares me witless. I can't protect him. I know that my darling boy, who already accepts without complaint so much discomfort, will one day also have to cross this huge obstacle alone.

I know that fear is important, an essential survival tool that triggers us to 'fight or flight' but in this helpless, nothing-I-can-do space it can be crushing: the unwanted, undermining anti-cheerleader. I have tried, exhausted myself with trying, to walk away from the fear, but one day at a time, even one inch at a time, it is too hard. I have had to find another way; I have had to learn to live with uncertainty.

This, though, *this* is the gift. I look at my son and he is beautiful: he shines with love and happiness. He is funny and joy-filled and cute beyond words and today, just for today, everything really is OK. Today everything is perfect and Felix is safe, planting dribbly kisses on my neck and promising to marry me one day. Today is good, more than good, and I have learned to enjoy it, to relish every second. It is so easy to throw today away, filling it with worries about a tomorrow that may never come.

This though, is the essence of parenting: for every glorious rush of pride, there is a dark and sickening fear and I seem to swing between the two at breakneck speed. I have discovered that Felix, for all his frailty, does not have the monopoly on my maternal anxiety; in fact in some ways I actually seem to lose less sleep over him than I do over the other two kids. Perhaps it's because his problems are so obvious and concrete: I can see them coming and can brace myself for the fight. With Joey and Evie, though, the future feels much more shadowy. I know that they will, like all of us, have their share of heartache but I have no idea where it will come from, or how deep will be the wound. I pray that I have given them whatever tools they need to deal with the inevitable slings and arrows of adulthood, and I try not to imagine that disaster lurks behind every door.

As I get older the months, and even years, whirl by so fast I am frequently dizzy with the speed of change. Children, *all* children, grow up and are gone in a heartbeat; and I will always be thankful that I have been taught to treasure that which is right under my nose.

~ 20 ~

Nobody said it would be easy. The road to here has already taken more unexpected twists and perilous detours than I could have imagined. I look back and can only be grateful that I never had the ability to look ahead. What would I have done, if I could have seen what was in store for me? I am sure that I would never have had the courage to choose this particular path: it has, in truth, been far harder than even my darkest imaginings. And yet, ah yes, along the way there have been some spectacular, awe-inspiring views. You struggle through dramas, clawing your bloody way over and around obstacles and then, suddenly, you stumble into a clearing and the sun hits you square in the face and, after all the darkness and the difficulty, a simple space of light and air feels as holy as a cathedral.

Getting this far has been epic; I feel like I have lived through several lifetimes already. I am so far away from that woman who lay on a hospital bed, in a darkened room, watching one, then two little heartbeats appear on a screen. I wonder, sometimes, what happened to her: what happens to all the people we no longer are? I think they pepper our lives with half-remembered, half-imagined perspectives, ghosts of our former selves. I look at Evie and Felix and I can see that everything they are, they are *now*. They absolutely sparkle with immediacy; existing fully in each moment, head back, arms open, engaged. But every move I make throws a flickering kaleidoscope of shadows, *tac-tac-tac* behind me softly, the essence of all the people I have been. Perhaps this is wisdom; the collective voice of our own past selves.

Of course, this begs the question 'who am I now?' Perhaps only hindsight can answer that; for today it is far easier to say who I am not. I am not a martyr and I'm definitely not a saint. I'm not particularly brave either, in direct contradiction to popular opinion. I am a woman that a load of stuff happened to, who managed not to drown. Every day, in thousands of ways, I hear 'I couldn't do it. I couldn't live the life you live, stand the things you stand, bear the load you bear' and I want to scream 'Yes, you could!' It's just a life; bits are hard, and bits are simple and I get up every morning and live it because it's my life. I didn't choose it, but I also don't ask 'why me?' Because it seems obvious to me that the real question, for all of us, should be 'why not me?'

This is where I am today: the slightly unsteady centre of a chaotic twenty-first century family. I don't *feel* like I'm in control of anything much, and it always strikes me as faintly miraculous, every time the whole shambolic creation manages to survive another day. I suppose what I do have, though, is a faith that I can survive whatever life throws at me. If experience has shown me anything, it is that I have the ability to climb out of a hole, however deep it is.

Everything has changed; my view of the world is as fundamentally altered as the world's view of me. Actually, the world seems like a kinder place these days: most people, I have found, really do want to do the right thing, the decent thing. In the past six years I have witnessed countless small acts of thoughtfulness and generosity from strangers, people who have crossed my path just fleetingly. Naturally there have been the others too, the selfish and the ignorant who shock you with their bigotry and unfairness, but they are actually pretty few and far between, and I am learning how to keep them out of my path. I am warned, by parents who have been on this road longer than I have, that the balance between positive and negative experiences will shift unfavourably as Felix gets older; people find a disabled child much more appealing than an adolescent with special needs. It worries me, of course, that one day Felix will no longer be 'cute' but I try not to dwell on it. I have learned that there will be plenty of time to worry about tomorrow's problems tomorrow; I don't need to throw away today on them. The future hasn't happened yet, and there is no guarantee that the future of my imagination will ever happen. And there, in that sentence, lies a dilemma.

Just after Felix was diagnosed with Nemaline Myopathy, I had a conversation with a friend about the life expectancy of people with different conditions. I was telling her that, unlike a classic muscular dystrophy, there was technically no shortening of lifespan with NM. There was a *tendency* for people with NM to become weaker over time, but this was more to do with a lack of exercise than with physical changes in the body. In fact, at least in theory, it was possible to prevent this weakening altogether, and keep the patient stable. I explained how this meant that we didn't have that awful sense of a clock ticking over Felix's head or of time running out; we simply didn't know how long he had. And then she said, 'Yes, but *he probably won't make very old bones*, will he?'

I've never forgotten those words (although, God knows, I've tried to) or the sense of their fundamental truth that hit me the moment I heard them. It's true, I don't know how long I've got with Felix: he probably *won't* make old bones but, then again, he might. I find this knowledge affects me much more than I would have ever imagined. It is hard, for example, to plan for a future that may never happen. I want to seize each moment with my son, to fill every day with fun and freedom and frivolity; but, of course, he has to go to school and have sensible bedtimes; he has to learn all those really important lessons, about how life doesn't always unfold exactly as you would wish it to. But a corner of my mind always wonders whether, if he should die in childhood, I will regret the battles over early nights and brushed teeth.

I also want to make sense of everything that has happened. I suppose that, more than anything, I want to be able to find meaning in all the pain, to know that the sadness had a purpose, that it all happened for a reason. There is an instinctive urge to find order in the chaos. I am essentially an optimist so I want to be able to see a force for good, a divine, benign hand shaping my life: I want to feel cared for. What was it all about, this huge adventure? The different pieces of the story fell together so specifically, it is hard to think of it as random. It was only because I had twins that our journey was made public; it was my fear of the unknown that pushed me to open my heart to strangers and Danny's job meant that we were early adopters of the internet for emotional support. I also wonder if Theo came just to hold Felix's hand? Did God, perhaps mindful of the hard journey ahead for little Felix, send a chaperone to settle him in and to help watch over him? Even my darling Theo's name, 'gift from God', seems curiously apt; I can never quite escape the thought that our sweet baby boy really was an angel. Perhaps, though, this is just a mother's heart speaking; don't we all see our children as magical and miraculous? Perhaps it is not surprising that I felt a spark of the divine in my Theo.

Acceptance is a continuing process, it's not the once-and-for-all thing that most people imagine. As Felix has grown, I have had to let go, one by one, of my dreams for him: talking, walking, eating, the list of things he cannot do grows longer every year. And each day I reaffirm my acceptance of my son and the life he has, and I push the darker thoughts and fears from my mind. Last year I went to Canada for the very first conference on Nemaline Myopathy, and I met dozens of other people who are living with this condition. People who I have been emailing for years were suddenly there in the flesh. The experience affected me powerfully in so many ways. I feel such bonds with these people: they truly are like family; our common heritage is etched into our very genes. To meet at last, to shake their hands and look into their eyes, felt good and right and easy. But there was also pain for me, confronted anew with the frailty of NM: I was shocked by how hard it was. When I look at Felix I see just him, my beautiful, perfect, glorious son. I see no broken body, kept alive by machines and fed by tubes; even now, just in the writing of these words, I cannot find my precious boy in such a description. In Canada, though, I saw the other, unfamiliar children, and I saw the Nemaline and the tubes and wires; it brought it home that this *was* my baby, as others see him. I was scared and shocked all over again. So, each day, I get up and renew my acceptance. I accept my son's disability, I accept the people in my house, I accept the life I've been given because I want to use my time and strength for living, not for fighting.

Not long ago, a friend came to see me because she was thinking of fostering a little boy on a ventilator; a child, in fact, not unlike Felix. She asked me what I thought, whether I would, in fact, recommend this life? The question took me by surprise: I had never been given a choice and I felt unable, at that time, to give her an answer. I think, though, that now I can. I would like to think that I *would* have had the imagination to choose this path but, in truth, I think I probably wouldn't have. I'm pretty sure I would have been too scared and too prejudiced to set out willingly on this journey, yet that would have been a huge and terrible loss. What I have today is so precious, and the harshness of the journey to get here just makes me value it even more.

* * *

Before I go to bed I check my children. In the kitchen I say goodnight to Joey as he, an ever-hungry teenage boy, rummages in the fridge; he'll still be up, hunched over a drawing or his computer, long after I am safely unconscious. In Evie's room I kiss her forehead and tuck her flung-out limbs back under the covers. She stirs slightly, and snuggles into her flowers blanket, thumb in mouth; the gentle *suck-suck-suck* noise makes me smile and I kiss her head again.

I go to kiss Felix goodnight. His carer sits across the darkened room, readying his bag for school. I kiss his half-closed sleeping fist, sticky with childhood. The rhythmic hum of the ventilator is hypnotic, drawing me in to the warm and womb-like space around my son. My stomach turns over in a rush of fear. I can't lose him, I can't lose him, dear God please don't take him from me. Tears prickle my eyes so I step back and draw breath. I shake the thought from my mind and push the fear back into its gated corner of my heart. I know it will escape again, it always does, but, for now, I am winning.

* * *

Life really is fragile. Not good, not bad, just life. All we ever have is the moment, here and now, and all we can ever do is live it. Live it with all our might: no half-arsed, half-measures but wholly, absolutely in each second. Taste it, touch it and then let it go.

There are things in my life that scare me, and there are things that make me want to dance and shout with joy. I have learned that, if I am to create something beautiful, I need all the colours. Sadness and loss are as much part of the spectrum as love and desire. This journey has, at times, been so hard that I have wondered if I would even survive it, days when grief consumed me so entirely I could not speak or stand or eat or feel. Now, though, the palette with which I paint my life is rich and full, with colours that are deep or bright, soft, pale, tender and brash. Each moment is a canvas and, if I want, can be a work of art drawn from the rainbow of my life.

Here I am then: face to the sun, arms open to the day, alive. I am smiling; I am ready; I choose life.

What's the worst that could happen?

appendices

nemaline myopathy

Felix was diagnosed with NM at nine months old, two months after Theo died. Had Theo not been an identical twin it is highly unlikely that we would ever have known what his condition was: he would have just been another child who died from an unknown condition, like so many others. Before the twins I, like most people, assumed that identifying diseases, disabilities and syndromes was a fairly straightforward area of medicine. I found out that, in fact, once you get away from relatively common disorders, you move rapidly into needle-in-a-haystack territory. In the disability parenting groups I have joined it seems that most of the children have no overall diagnosis, just a list of symptoms and attributes: getting a name for Felix's condition was, in itself, a major victory.

Nemaline Myopathy is a neuromuscular disorder. The name, nemaline, refers to the thread-like rods that appear in the muscles of the patient. These rods prevent the muscle from functioning properly, making the patient physically weak: in the most severe cases the muscles are so weak that movement is almost completely absent. NM is often classified as a muscular dystrophy, indeed the Muscular Dystrophy Association (MDA) lists NM as one of the conditions under its 'umbrella'. However, there is a key difference between a myopathy and a dystrophy: while a myopathy is any disease of the muscle (myo=muscle; pathos=disease), a dystrophy is actually a special class of myopathy, characterised by progressive muscle degeneration. Nemaline Myopathy is known as a non-dystrophic myopathy and is often (but not always) non-progressive.

NM can affect almost every muscle (particularly skeletal muscle, which is responsible for movement and force) and there is a huge variation in the way it manifests in different patients. In Felix his respiratory muscles are very weak and so he needs help to breathe effectively. Respiration actually has two functions: to get oxygen into the body, and to get carbon dioxide (CO_2) out of the body. Felix can breathe unaided for several hours but his breaths are very shallow and he is unable to effectively get rid of his CO_2. It is this, CO_2 poisoning, that would ultimately kill him if he was left without his ventilator for an extended period. His oral muscles are also profoundly affected by his NM: this makes it very difficult for him to articulate words clearly. His speech, even for those of us who know him extremely well, is exception-ally difficult to understand. We are currently looking at commu-nication aids for him and he will, almost certainly, end up with an artificial voice. His weak muscles also make oral feeding unsafe for Felix. He has great difficulty swallowing, it is not a reflexive act for him, and he is unable to properly protect his airway so, when food or liquid is in his mouth, there is always a risk that some will find its way to his lungs. For these reasons he receives all his nutrition via a tube directly into his stomach (his gastros-tomy). He also requires regular suctioning in order to clear saliva and other secretions from his mouth and tracheostomy. Felix uses a power wheelchair; he cannot stand or walk at all and even sitting unaided becomes difficult for him very quickly. He has very little strength in his hands and we have found that, even on toys designed for babies, buttons are often too hard for him to push.

As Felix gets physically bigger, there are some aspects of his life that become more difficult, but he is also learning to take responsibility for some of his own care, helping with suctioning and his monthly trach changes. He will, however, always require full-time support and will need to have carers for the rest of his life. He has never spent a single night unmonitored or alone, and that is unlikely to change.

There are currently several laboratories internationally work-ing on therapies specifically for NM as well as other neuromuscu-lar conditions. Genetic and stem-cell research is yielding some promising results for many diseases, including NM. Unfortunately they are still a long way from any kind of 'cure', or even effective therapy; we have learned to accept that Felix's condition will almost certainly never improve. Much more encouraging is the way that medical technology is evolving and improving all the time. Ventilators and suction machines are getting smaller and lighter, wheelchairs are getting more sophisticated and computers are giving new abilities and freedoms to even the most profoundly disabled people. I believe that it is the ongoing development of technology that will ultimately have the biggest impact on Felix's quality of life.

online communities

It's incredible to think that when I discovered that I was pregnant for a third time I didn't even have an email address. I wasn't unusual in any way; few people had non-work email at that time and online communities were still really in their infancy. What is even more remarkable is that this was not very long ago, less than eight years, though it feels like a lifetime.

Email, the internet; an incredible, invisible mesh: a network of relationships, strangers connecting in a thousand ways, criss-crossing oceans and continents; and more than capable of bearing the weight of one frightened and heavy heart. I can hardly imagine how different this story might have been without my virtual life. From emotional support to raw medical facts, my feet have been guided at every step by the collective wisdom of thousands of strangers. This is the modern world: there is no longer any such thing as isolation.

Even now, say the word 'internet' and for many people it conjures up visions of inescapable pornography; lonely geeks writing smart-arsed weblogs; school kids surfing natural history sites for homework projects and disenchanted teenagers spewing impotent rage. Sometimes people will mention the massive and powerful commerce of eBay and Amazon and, if pushed, most will recognise that the democratising of knowledge has been a good thing, affecting daily life in countless small but significant ways. The amount of knowledge I have at my fingertips is staggering, from the weather forecast for a small town on the other side of the planet, to the last thirty winners of the Grand National: it's all just seconds away and, without doubt, this has had huge implications for the medical profession as both doctors and patients have had access to vast tracts of previously undiscovered information. But the great unsung function of the internet is the way that it brings people together.

The Twins List was, of course, my introduction to the internet and the concept of a virtual community. Virtual communities are very similar to physical ones in many ways; they have in-crowds and popularity queens, wise 'elders', try-hards, eccentrics and clowns; they also have rules, both explicit and implicit, in-jokes and, inevitably, conflict. There were also, I found, real parallels with the twelve-step groups I had been involved in: the principle of anonymity in both kinds of group allowed for a degree of intimacy to develop that was unmatched in most real-world communities. At a time when we are all less and less likely to get to know our actual neighbours, when physical communities are becoming less important, these virtual communities seem to have blossomed, as though fulfilling some fundamental human need for casual friendships and group identity.

The internet is home to countless communities, though; when it was no longer appropriate for me to be a member of the Twins List, there was no shortage of fitting replacements. As I surfed around, following recommendations, joining and leaving groups, I learned that I had to be pretty discriminating about where I signed up, if I wasn't to be overwhelmed by an unmanageable email load.

My first post-Twins List venture was into the bereavement communities. I joined a couple of groups that were specifically aimed at women who had lost a twin or higher multiple before, at or soon after birth. Pretty much all of the other mothers in the group had lost their babies through either miscarriage or extreme prematurity; my loss of seven-month-old, full-term baby Theo made me something of an oddity but, nevertheless, it was a relief to meet people who understood some of the very particular anguish of losing a twin.

I stayed around the bereavement lists for about a year, and I will always be grateful for the support I got there. I have no doubt that having a safe space to share my desperate grief, in the early days after Theo's death, helped me enormously to process the sorrow. Eventually, though, it started to feel self-indulgent and I knew it was time to leave. I didn't need to hear that I would 'never get over it'; I needed to hear that I could and, indeed, *would* recover. As with the Twins List, the decision to go was mine alone: I was assured that I would always have a place there if I wanted to return, but it felt right to leave. I wanted to be looking forward, not back, and I felt increasingly out of step with the other mothers: it was time to go.

By the time I was ready to move on from the bereavement lists

I had already started to connect with the next stage of my online existence: the medical and disability parenting communities. Some of the biggest changes in healthcare, particularly in the relationship between doctor and patient, have come from the widespread use of the internet. Patients are no longer passive recipients of a doctor's wisdom and judgement: they are actively researching, checking and questioning, able partners in their own care. Getting a second opinion, once an unwieldy and time-consuming process, is very often just a click away. Doctors are no longer the sacred holders of The Knowledge: nowadays we can all be experts. It's not just about who has access to information either; by bringing together people with rare or isolating conditions you allow comparisons and, sometimes, important discoveries are made. Nemaline myopathy, Felix's condition, is very rare and the wide variation in severity means that even if, and this is unlikely, a doctor treating him *has* come across the condition before, the case is likely to have manifested very differently. Online, however, scattered across the globe, I have found a handful of children whose NM is very like my son's. Corresponding with these families has enabled me to build a picture of the disease and, most importantly, to identify which of Felix's many quirks are actually caused by NM, and which are just his own funny little idiosyncrasies. Now, when I accompany Felix to one of his numerous hospital check-ups, I am very often the real expert on his health, bringing with me news of recent research breakthroughs, and new treatments and therapies to try.

There are hundreds of thousands of medical and disability-related email groups on the internet, each with its own remit, tone and character. Over the years I have passed through a number of groups, moving on from those that didn't feel like a 'good fit'. I have ended up with an actively participating membership of two or three, and I 'lurk' in a couple of others.

Our-Kids is a list for parents of children with disabilities, *all* disabilities. I joined the group a couple of months after the twins were born, once it started to become clear that there was more to their problems than just being a bit small and weedy. It was a real education, smashing thirty-odd years of wilful ignorance into a million pieces. It was *Our-Kids* that first opened my eyes to a world and a culture I had never previously noticed. The group helped me through the early days of guilt and acceptance, and the warmth and humour I found there told me that things were not so bad really. Most of all, I learned that there really is always someone worse off than you: people whose children's disabilities made Felix's look like a badly grazed knee; people coping with a child's terminal condition; families who have suffered multiple losses and still had more to come.

I have learned so much from the families on *Our-Kids*, both good and bad. I have followed people's stories and their coping strategies. I have seen parents who have to fight every day just to get the most basic needs of their child met, and I have been awed by those who remain upbeat and energised in the face of such relentless opposition. I have seen the other way too: parents consumed with grief and anger, raging against a world that won't help them, unable to see that it is often their own fury that makes that world want to keep them at arm's length. Other people's lives, stories that can guide me through dark times or, equally important, show me the life I don't want.

I joined the Nemaline List when Felix got his diagnosis. Compared to *Our-Kids* or even the Twins List, it is a tiny group made up of parents like me, as well as older kids and adults who have NM themselves. This group feels like family: it's not just the incredible facial similarities of people with NM, or even the camaraderie that comes from knowing that we are linked by something so rare, it is the powerful commonality of our experience that bonds us more than anything else. Knowing that others are dealing with the same issues and fears makes the journey so much less daunting. There is a shared history and, in a group of people categorised as medically fragile there will, inevitably, be losses. As a group there is a collective bracing as autumn becomes winter, and a palpable sense of relief as spring kicks in. We have been through so much together: terrible tragedies, anxious pregnancies and great triumphs of both medicine and will. Newcomers join us, sometimes as parents struggling to understand the blow fate has dealt them; sometimes it is an adult with NM, who has spent a whole lifetime being 'different' and is meeting others like themselves for the first time. For all of us, newcomers and old-timers, however we are connected to nemaline, it is emotional and affirming, retelling our stories and recognising our own lives in the tales of others. We are a close-knit and supremely knowledgeable group. As individual patients it is difficult to be influential, but collectively we have a voice which is loud enough to be heard. Through raising money and making connections with the leading researchers in NM, we are no longer impotent; we can be part of the process that shapes nemaline's future.

Empowerment. It may be a long time before we really see the

full effects of the internet on the disabled community; perhaps only when a whole generation has been born and grown up with it will its influence become apparent. Already, though, I can see so many ways that times have changed and I am grateful beyond measure that Felix is right at the forefront of this brave new electronic dawn. Disability, however it manifests, is essentially isolating. Some people communicate differently, some think differently; there are a thousand ways to build barriers between people. For most people with disabilities, the simple, human desire to touch others is thwarted in countless physical, emotional and social ways. And if you are isolated how do you organise? How do you change things if you are alone and trapped in your own tiny world? Together people can change things: a million lone voices can never compete with one voice, a million strong. Through the internet, people with disabilities are finding each other, they are organising, and they are making that one voice, loud and clear.

* * *

I am wary of putting a long list of websites and groups in this book. Times and technology change so quickly it is inevitable that some of the information would be out of date almost immediately. For this reason, I am listing only the Twins List, the Nemaline website and *Our-Kids*. There are countless groups out there, and they range from the all-encompassing to the ultra-specialised. Finding the right one is often going to be a matter of individual choice. Do you want a group that is technical and informative? Or are you looking for emotional support; or even comic relief? How busy is the group? If it's a very big group you may find the volume of posts so high that you rarely have time to read it. Word of mouth (or rather 'word of keyboard') is the best way of finding groups. Join one of the big catch-all groups (like the Twins List) and ask listmates for other, more specific, recommendations (on home schooling, for example).

If you are interested in a particular condition or disability, a basic Google search should point you at specialist websites, and many of these will have an email group attached. For more recreational interests, Yahoo Groups is home to thousands of groups on just about any subject you can think of. Parenting, music, sports, arts, hobbies, politics...the list is almost endless and, with so many groups to choose from, almost everyone can find a community to suit them.

The Twins List – http://www.twinslist.org/

Nemaline Myopathy – http://www.davidmcd.btinternet.co.uk/

Our-Kids – http://www.our-kids.org/

Yahoo Groups – http://groups.yahoo.com/

in memory of costas berou
1945–2005

When I was halfway through writing this book, my father died. He had non-Hodgkin's lymphoma, a type of cancer which, despite the best efforts of his doctors, finally overwhelmed his system in February 2005. He was just fifty-nine years old. His death presented me with a dilemma: although my father doesn't feature in this book very much at all, the references that do appear don't show him in a particularly good light. I was very tempted to go back over those pieces and rewrite them with more generosity but, in the end, I felt that this would be dishonest. I have left the book as it was originally intended: the parts about my father are a true reflection of how I felt and the relationship we had. However, I didn't want to leave it like that. My father, for all his faults, deserves a better memorial, and I would want him to have one.

My relationship with my father has always been complicated but, for much of my life, I have been angry with him. As a man he had many fine qualities: he was a good friend, he was a great boss and he could be a lot of fun. He was living in Cyprus when he died and I, along with Danny, flew out to join my siblings at his bedside for his final days. After his death, we went back to the house and spent some time looking at old photographs of our dad in his glory days. He worked on cruise ships his whole life, starting out as a lowly waiter and working his way up to vice-president of a cruise line. The photographs showed him extraordinarily handsome and utterly carefree, standing on a beach in Acapulco, cocktail in hand; or sharp-suited on a piazza in Rome, a cigarette dangling from his lip, in the days when it was cool to smoke. And there were always girls; *lots* of girls. He had a real eye for the ladies, and they loved him right back. Occasionally one would get a bit more serious, and I'd be introduced to another sweet-faced honey, who would go to great lengths to bond with me, presumably in the (mistaken) belief that this would secure their place in my father's heart. In fact one of my earliest memories of him is a trip to the park when I was around five or six years old. As we walked across the grass, my dad noticed two pretty girls coming towards us. As they neared, he whispered down to me 'don't call me daddy'. I got older, but my dad's girlfriends didn't. By the time I was twenty, the age gap between me and them had all but vanished, which led to some surreal moments and occasional discomfort.

My father was born in the headquarters of the Cypriot Communist Party, and a sense of duty to the workers remained throughout his life. He was worshipped by the people who worked for him; no matter how high up in management he went, he never lost sight of the needs of those at the bottom of the pyramid. He fought ferociously for them, for better pay, better conditions, just for the right to be treated with respect and, in return, they gave him their all. He worked hard, he looked after his crew and he got the very best out of them; whether as an employer, or as an employee, you really wanted to have him on your team. He was a very intelligent man as well as a compassionate one; he intuitively understood how to motivate a team and he was incredibly loyal.

But, despite apparently having all the necessary qualities in abundance, for most of his life his biggest failing was as a father; although he actually did, eventually, get his act together. For me and (to a slightly lesser degree) Antony, he was largely absent, desperately unreliable and continuously disappointing. He just didn't seem to have it in him to *commit* to a child. When Katerina was born my dad, realising that this was his last chance to be a decent parent, finally got his act together and made certain that, for his youngest daughter at least, he was always available with financial and emotional support, right up to packing her off to university shortly before his death.

The day he died, as all three of his children sat around his hospital bed, watching the life ebb out of him, he mustered all his energy into one of his last coherent moments and told us, 'I want to have fun; I'm not having *fun*.' For sixty years his life had been about the pursuit of fun above almost everything else. Things that were not fun, like being a parent, were abandoned; out of sight meant out of mind for him. Bad news was avoided or ignored: the doctors had been telling him to stop drinking, stop smoking, to look after himself physically; but where was the fun in that? Then came the cancer, not fun at all; and this time he couldn't run away from it. Sixty years is not a long life, but my dad probably managed to cram enough fun into his to last most people eighty years. He used up all his fun too quickly, and then he had nothing to live for.

My father was not a bad man; he knew that he'd been a lousy parent and he carried a ton of guilt about it. He just wanted to be happy, but he could never really understand the difference between happiness and fun. In the end he had a lot of fun but I don't think he ever really knew happiness; that was his tragedy. I went to sit by his death bed hoping that perhaps, finally, we would connect but, of course, we couldn't. I think that my father loved me as much as he could, in the only way he knew, and I am grateful for that.